Root Root Root For The Home Teams

*A Chicago Fan's Odyssey to Find
the Meaning of Life Through Sport*

By Tom Dobrez

Published by

Across My Aprils

For more information:
Across My Aprils
1135 Golfview ln
Flossmoor, IL 60422

ISBN 979-8-9876988-1-5 (Hardcover)
ISBN 979-8-9876988-0-8 (Paperback)
ISBN 979-8-9876988-2-2 (e-book)

Published in The United States Of America

Disclaimer
This work depicts actual events in the life of the author as truthfully as recollection permits and/or can be verified by research. Occasionally, dialogue consistent with the character or nature of the person speaking has been supplemented. All persons within are actual individuals; there are no composite characters. It is the author's wish to respect all those involved and no malice is intended.

Book cover design: Katie Sullivan
Typesetting design: Spiro Books
Back cover photo: Only known photo of author's mother attending a Chicago sport's team event. She is surrounded by her seven children.

*To my wife Edie,
My Penelope on this odyssey*

"There are untold riches in the depths of this game."

JASON BENETTI
HOMEWOOD-FLOSSMOOR HIGH SCHOOL CLASS OF 2001
CHICAGO WHITE SOX PLAY BY PLAY ANNOUNCER

TABLE OF CONTENTS

PRE-GAME

Take Me Out To The Ball Game

You never forget your first game,
especially when they forget you.

Six days after the assassination of the Rev. Dr. Martin Luther King Jr. and four days before my seventh birthday, the Chicago White Sox would open their 1968 season at home in Comiskey Park against the Cleveland Indians. The city was still simmering from the King murder and there was concern that a visit to the park on Chicago's Southside might prove dangerous.

It would also be the opening day of the National Guard's presence in the city that summer. In the post killing atmosphere, rioters had taken to the streets on Chicago's West Side in the Lawndale and Austin neighborhoods. As city blocks burned, firefighters struggled to reach the structures to extinguish them. Rioters greeted them with bottles, rocks and occasional sniper fire. Over 6,000 Reserve troops were called in to restore calm. By Monday, April 8th, twelve people died, random gunfire wounded a firefighter, and 170 buildings burnt.

None of this seemed to bother my dad, who was coming into his own. He was entering the prime of his life. John Francis Dobrez was a first generation American. Born during the Great Depression to immigrant parents from Croatia, he spent much of his youth moving houses and working late hours. As his father struggled to stay employed, the family changed homes frequently. However, on this Opening Day of the major league baseball season, he found himself at home.

My dad had overcome his feeble beginnings and minimal education to become a man in full. The industrial chemical manufacturing business he started celebrated its first decade of success. He moved his growing family into a custom-built home in Flossmoor, Illinois. A community that would lead me to my future wife, Edie, and remain my hometown, five plus decades later. My dad would die in the house I now live in. On this April day in 1968, hope did spring eternal for him and his family.

My dad invited his brothers and their children to join my two older brothers and me for a day at the ballpark. The plan called for a dozen cousins and uncles to meet at my Uncle Dick's farm-style house in the Chicago south suburb of Oak Lawn. We arrived thirty minutes before we would need to depart to Comiskey Park or as we pronounced it, 'CoMINski' for the first pitch. We parked in the driveway along the side of the house in front of the detached garage.

As the others began arriving, I slipped away to check out what cool stuff my cousins might have in their garage. I became engrossed in the treasures hidden in this solitary space. Something occupied my restless mind as I hung out, alone in the garage. For how long, I am uncertain. What I am certain of, it was far too long.

When I emerged from the garage, I noticed a strange scene. The driveway, teeming with cars a moment ago, was now down to one red coupe, my aunt's car. The rest of the driveway was empty. My family's woody station wagon and my uncle's cars were gone. I felt bewildered. Five decades later, I can still recall the place's still-ness and the emptiness. Perplexed, I took cautious steps toward the house. I hadn't put the clues together yet.

I walked up the white wooden staircase that led to the back door, the family entrance of the house, and slowly eased my head first into the kitchen. In a room, where moments ago, there was a cacophony of cousins and uncles, now there was starkness. Nothing, no one. I heard a noise in the next room and took cau-tionary steps into the house's emptiness. I poked my head into the living room and made eye contact with a person sitting calmly there. The woman ejected from her seat and lurch towards me. It was my Aunt Ruth. Her eyes grew from their loving softness to raging irises the size of Wile E. Coyote's as he braced himself from the blow of a 1000-pound anvil. She grabbed my arms and looked me in the face with care, concern, and probably some inner rage. "What are you doing here?"

I didn't know. I'm sure my face relayed as much to her. Then, it sank in. They had left me behind.

Meanwhile, as relayed later that night, the three cars of uncles and cousins arrived at 35th and Shields. My dad, a sergeant in the First Cavalry Division that fought in Korea, summoned his military discipline and directed all the family members present to form a line to get their tickets. He handed each one their cherished voucher — an opening day pass to see our home team White Sox. As the last of the clan received his ticket, my dad turned in disbelief and confusion. He had one too many tickets. The circumstances demanded a roll call. As each family member counted off, the mistake became apparent. The youngest of the bunch was missing, causing panic only a loving parent knows.

As the alarm set in, my dad looked for a pay phone. There was none nearby. Park security told him the only phone was inside the ballpark. He instructed everyone to enter the game. Once inside, he called Aunt Ruth. She eased his pain as she assured him I was fine. My clan stayed and watched the game, probably feeling a mixture of excessive guilt and relief.

Back in the suburbs, I was being treated by Aunt Ruth as if I was the first in line for the throne. Having realized the magnitude of the situation, she shifted into service mode. She did everything she could to divert my attention away from the painful reality of being abandoned. Soon, the house smelled of vanilla and chocolate. The smell of childhood - Nestle Toll House cookies. We watched the game together on a 12-inch black-and-white TV.

That day, I forged a kinship with my aunt that has lasted for over 50 years. As I write this on her 90th birthday, April 13, I reflect on the kindness she bestowed upon me. She filled the day with compassion and grace. She had planned a day off to enjoy the quietness without the chaos that usually surrounded her. Suddenly, a seven-year-old moseys into her den, his face filled with anxiety, and her response is to console and feed the young boy. Her reaction speaks of the sacrifices of motherhood. In that moment, I understood compassion.

The White Sox lost that opening day game in front of a mere 7,756 brave souls, eleven of which shared my last name. They didn't win their first game until 15 days later, starting the season off at 0-10. They used three managers to lead them to ninth place. The city of Chicago also continued to descend into despair in the summer of 1968. Even more upheaval followed the King riots at the infamous 1968 Democratic National Convention. When National Guardsmen returned in larger numbers to quell over 10,000 protestors. So began my rocky relationship with Chicago professional sports.

On that opening day, my loving aunt helped me overcame being left behind. For the rest of my life, the closeness of family and friends would temper the waves of disappointment that come with rooting for the home team. Year after year, watching my teams crushed my soul. However, being with friends or family provided soothing relief. That day, Aunt Ruth helped me see the sunshine of the day through the love she shone on me. I would need to cling to that comfort many times through six decades of following Chicago sports. While I couldn't always rely on the teams to provide unbridled joy, being with friends and family was often the elixir that kept me emotionally afloat.

This memoir is primarily the story of the opening days and big games I didn't miss. On the surface, these are the stories of being in the stands for some of Chicago's greatest sports moments. Three years later, my dad more than made up for his opening day blunder by taking me to the first of my Chicago championship moments. Starting a good fortune streak that makes up the structure of this story. At everyone of those crowning games, there was someone by my side, enjoying the moment. It's the emotional story of memories shared with people I know intimately and the thou-sands, if not millions, I have never met but with whom I share the bond of following team sports in a big-league city.

Sports are the lifeblood coursing through the veins of its citi-zens that make a modern-day city come alive. A tale of emotions that make up the fabric of a town connected by its games. Sports capture much of what makes us human. Resiliency in the face of utter defeat is a key capacity of any fan. In Chicago, it seems to be a badge of honor.

As fans, we grow together. The mutual agony and ecstasy unite us. The games are occasionally poetry and often vulgar. It's our team there, the home team. It becomes our lives. Like in many cities across the world, fans identify with their teams. Here, we are Da Fans.

Together, we wrestle with the heartache of our team's seasons and the moral ambiguity of having sport stars as heroes. Whether it's as a distraction from the world's bigger uncontrollable events or a means to celebrate a special moment, being at the game is a chance to nourish your soul while you learn a bit about the world, family, and yourself. This book is what it felt like to be there. It's also what it means to be rooted in a family and in a place.

Root For The White Sox

If They Don't Win, It's A Shame

1st INNING

One of the oldest rules in Major League Baseball is Rule 6.09. In the Spring 2015 Baseball Research Journal, historian Richard Hershberger suggests the rule's origins date back to 1796 to an obscure German book on children's games. More recently, we can find the rule in what baseball buffs call the Knickerbocker Rules, established in 1845 by William R. Wheaton and William H. Tucker of the Knickerbocker Base Ball Club.

The rule, according to Hershberger, survives today "as an oddball vestige of an earlier age." He readily admits it's a "peculiar rule," fittingly adding, "on rare, magical occasions, the rule matters."

The White Sox playoff drive of 2005 was certainly rare, often magical, and it all mattered. None more so than Game 2 of the American League Championship Series (ALCS) when rule 6.09

came into play when Chicago White Sox catcher, A. J. Pierzynski, reached base on a dropped third strike.

A 160 years after the Knickerbocker rule, The Los Angeles Angels of Anaheim, a team caught between two cities, was coming into Chicago for the best of seven ALCS with the White Sox. The Sox hadn't been this far in the playoffs since 1983 two years before I married my wife Edie. Since that time, we married, made our home in Flossmoor, and had three children, Becca (at the time 16), Buddy (14) and Tommy (11).

The Angels flew into town late on October 10 after defeating the New York Yankees in Game 5 of the best of five in Anaheim. The Sox were looking to take advantage of a tired team and get the jump on the series. That didn't happen. In front of 40,659 fans at what was then called U.S. Cellular Field, the Angels surprised the home team, 3-2, in the series opener.

As a season ticket holder that year, I had passed on tickets to the game so I could secure five tickets to Game 2 and take my family. Years of baseball failure were about to coalesce into a dream family moment. For the game, Tommy had taken a giant foam fist, initially meant as a Halloween costume of The Hulk, and painted it black. Then he fancied a stylish script S-O-X on the back of the hand in white. This was no flimsy Number 1 foam finger; this was a one-of-a-kind Fist of Power. Black Sox muscle. It was a hit amongst fans as well as the roaming stadium TV cameras that featured it on the Jumbotron multiple times.

As my son repeatedly pumped his oversized Sox fist, Mark Buehrle was reveling in another of his pitching gems. However, one mistake looked costly. Through nine innings, Number 56 had allowed only one run: a fifth-inning homer by Robb Quinlan, whoever he was. That hit had tied the game 1-1. The Sox went one, two, and almost three in a row in the bottom of the ninth. But then, an odd thing happened on A. J. Pierzynski's way back to the dugout. A. J. had missed Kelvim Escobar's wicked pitch in the dirt for strike three. He slowly moved to return to the dugout, where he'd put his tools of ignorance on to start the tenth. Then he had a second thought. He headed for first base, thinking there may have been a dropped third strike.

Pierzynski claimed he knew what he was doing. When questioned further by reporter Teddy Greenstein, A. J. recalled a similar situation from a year previous. Pierzynski was catching for the San Francisco Giants in 2004. A pitcher for the Boston Red Sox, Bronson Arroyo, who also was a Little League teammate of A. J., was batting. Arroyo struck out on a pitch in the dirt. He walked back to the dugout and then changed his mind. He ran to first base and was called safe by the home umpire. Pierzynski and his teammates argued to no avail. Arroyo was safe. A. J. lost the argument but cataloged the moment for future reference. A year later, A. J. would tap that memory bank with great dividends.

After some debate, the umpire ruled Pierzynski safe at first as he determined that former White Sox player now Angels' catcher Josh Paul did not catch the ball cleanly. With a 'nothing-is-more-important-than-this-moment' attitude, A. J. went for broke and broke the Angels' backs. In the live TV broadcast, Tim McCarver says, "This might be the best thing for instant replay." (Three years later, MLB would become the last of the four major North American sports to use instant replay). But for now, the play stood. Pierzynski was safe, and the Sox were still alive in the ninth.

Manager Ozzie Guillén immediately substituted Pierzynski for pinch runner Pablo Ozuna, who continued to rattle the Angels by stealing second base on the next pitch. The next hitter, Joe Crede, smashed one off the wall, scoring Ozuna, and pandemonium erupted through the park on 35th Street. The Sox had tied the series. They had a complete game victory for Buehrle. They had pulled a rabbit out of the hat, and the Sox Hulk fist pumped with exuberance. Their improbable run had started with a most arcane rule. Magical.

The series would move to Anaheim for Game 3. The Sox sucked on the West Coast. There had been so many nights I stayed up late, watching Sox games that ended in misery after midnight Central time. They'd lose series after series in Oakland, Anaheim, and Seattle. It seemed Midwesterners couldn't stand the West Coast heat. As a result, they headed out to California with low expectations. We were looking for one win on the road to bring the series back home. We didn't know at the time that the next game the Sox would play in Chicago would be the first World Series game in four plus decades. But we are not there yet.

I was traveling West on the same day as the White Sox. My plane stopped in Denver; theirs was continuing another 1000 miles to Orange County. I was planning on attending an NFL football game between the Denver Broncos and the New England Patriots in a sky box suite. It was one of the marquee games on the league's schedule. A matchup of two elite teams. It was one of those 'Games of the Century' they hold yearly. A tough ticket, indeed; however, I had one reserved in luxury. I was Billy Lynn, getting ready for his long halftime walk.

Three months earlier, I received an invitation to the game from Bill Marlin, a partner in a law firm. In August, he emailed Dave Wagner and me. Inviting us to enjoy the game from the company suite. It was too sweet to turn down. I responded "yes" to the evite with one small caveat. "As long as the White Sox are not in the playoffs."

With the invitation accepted and the fine print disclaimer, which only my lawyer friend himself could later appreciate, we set our travel agendas accordingly. Dave would travel from Boston where he lived in the house his mother grew up in. Notwithstanding his Massachusetts' roots, Dave was born in Chicago's south suburbs and became a fast friend of mine in high school. Once on a whim, I told him I was preparing to drive back to college the next day, he said "I'll go with you." Which doesn't sound like much until you realize I went to school at Texas A&M, 1000 miles away from home and I wasn't planning on bringing him back unless he stayed the semester. Dave was always game for a game or, to be honest, for anything. Dave invented the word "Yes." He was a man of resources, with an indelible smile, a penchant for the ladies, and a "Sure, let's do that" attitude; a friend who was only ever in need of a good time. Dave would meet us in Denver.

I owned a few radio stations in the mountains of Colorado, so any trip to Denver offered the opportunity to double dip. Along with some fellowship, I could conduct a little business. I'd fly out a day early, knock off some work-related tasks and then settle in Bill's comfortable home in Denver's outskirts. I scheduled a few days of overtime in Denver to attend to a couple more business obligations on the Monday following the Bronc's game. But first, I was ready for a weekend of the usual debauchery, which typically included whisky, beers, lies, and laughs—lots of laughs.

With the series tied at one game each, the Sox sent Jon Garland to the mound in Anaheim. He was brilliant. His complete game followed Buehrle's for the first back-to-back complete games in the playoffs since Tommy John and Bruce Kison had done it for the California Angels twenty-three years earlier. More critical for us fans of the silver and black, we had a two games to one lead in the best-of-seven series. I was in Edwards, Colorado, watching the game alone. Looking ahead, I realized the Sox could clinch the AL pennant in Game 5 on Sunday. I was worried that my planned presence at the Broncos' game would conflict with their schedule. I held my breath and reasoned that I was expecting too much for the Sox to roll through the Angels, who had a potent lineup. With the Sox' dismal record on the West Coast, it seemed beyond wishful thinking. If the Sox split the remaining games in Anaheim, they'd return to win the pennant before the home crowd. I had tickets for Game 6 presenting a best-case scenario. Then I thought, "Let's just get this thing over with."

On Saturday morning, I made the two-hour drive from my condo in Edwards near Vail to Bill's house in Denver for a barbecue. Game 4 was that night. Dave and I would sleep at Bill's with a leisurely Sunday morning planned before heading to the football game. As we chowed on chicken, we settled in front of Bill's TV to watch Freddy Garcia start for the White Sox. Meanwhile, A. J. Pierzynski was preparing to get into the middle of it all again.

But first, a sidebar on my friend and bar member, 'Bill-esquire', as I sometimes refer to him. A lawyer by trade, a friend by nature, and a soul at peace. Bill tolerates sports. He understands the tribalistic appeal of team affinity, but he prefers live music to a regular season game in any sport. Raised in a small Illinois town with frequent moves as an Air Force brat, he never settled long enough in a single place to develop a strong attachment to a single team or sport. His allegiances were up for rent. He could get behind a Colorado Avalanche drive for a Stanley Cup and find joy in a White Sox triumph. Yet, he had his limits.

With his casual interest in sports, Bill understood where these playoffs stood. He also knew he had planned a special day in the Broncos' sky box for Dave and me. We sat in Bill's living room, watching the Sox take a 3-0 lead on a Paul Konerko blast in the first. Things were becoming interesting. Things got all A. J.'d up again in the second. Steve Finley was batting for the Angels with runners on first and third. Finley swung and grounded a ball into play. He took off for first, then looked back and yelled to the home plate ump that his bat had hit the catcher's mitt. The catcher was, you guessed it, A. J. Pierzynski. Finley screamed, then realized the ball was in play and no catcher interference call was coming; he raced down to first. He was late. The Sox had turned a double play on Finley by a step. Had he not turned to protest the interference call, he more than likely would have been safe, and the Angels would still be at-bat with one run scored. Instead, the inning ended with a no-call, no run. For the record, the bat hit the mitt. So life is determined by human decisions. Well, that is the way of the world.

Garcia finished the third complete game in a row with an 8-2 victory for the Chi-Sox, who now were on the brink of their first AL pennant since 1959, two years before I was born. A decision was pending. Game 5 was to be played the next night in Anaheim. It was the same day the Broncos were hosting the Patriots. I was sure of what I needed to do. All I needed was an accomplice and an out.

The thought seemed to hit Dave, my White Sox blood brother, and me at the same time. What will it take to get to Anaheim in time for the game? Is it even feasible? Could we fly there and get tickets to see the Sox clinch? There were a lot of variables. The only certainty seemed to be we had to go. We were confident we could overcome any logistical challenges. Bill, meanwhile, was a different story. He had been so gracious by inviting us into his home for the weekend. On top of his hospitality was his invite to join him at a premiere NFL game in a suite, the likes of which we may never have the privilege of seeing a game from again. A once-in-a-life-time football game. Or so they say.

I'll tell you what once in a lifetime is. It's a shot for the home team to make it to the World Series. When you grow up in a city with few championships over six-plus decades, the opportunity to witness glory arrive and frustration end is rare. The NFL seems to have games of the century all the time. But a chance to see one's beloved White Sox clinch a seat on the ship—The World Series— is something that had not happened in the first 44 years of my life. And here I was, 1000 miles away from that possibility. I had to maneuver; I had to move. I had to follow A. J.'s lead. Get the moment right. Do everything to win. I had to look into it, at the very least.

I hurried to Bill's laundry room, which he had converted into a makeshift office in the days when home computing was evolving. Like most, it was a utility in the back of one's house for accessing information, like an electronic library in one's home. Bill had an Internet connection, and I knew how to get on American Airlines' website. (It still works today, aa.com.) I was searching for flights to Los Angeles in secret. Dave and I didn't want to broach the idea with Bill just yet. We had to be sure we could pull this off. The funny thing is when you are in Denver, coming from Chicago or

Boston, you think you are next door to California. Nope, there is still almost half a continent to go.

I found an early Sunday morning flight to LAX with two seats available. The price was reasonable for a round trip that brought us back to Denver on Monday morning. Dave had a subsequent flight back to Boston booked already, and I was staying over a couple of days in Denver. I had business meetings with clients flying to Denver on Monday afternoon. The plan seemed reasonable. I turned to Dave, who was looking over my shoulder. I spoke no word. He said, "Book it."

"What about Bill? What do we tell him? How do we explain this to him?"

Dave pondered a moment and said, "The email."

Right away, I knew what he was talking about. I had covered my ass in advance. I had qualified my presence as subject to the White Sox being in the playoffs. When I wrote the email, I did not expect a potential conflict nor ever thought it would happen with me already in Denver, less than 24 hours from kickoff. Then again, not so sure, A. J. figured he'd have a dropped third strike opportunity he would remember for the rest of his life, either. But both of us were ready for it.

I booked the flights and steeled my resolve as Dave and I returned to the family room to address Bill.

"Uh, Bill. Do you remember that email I sent you when you invited us to this game?" I began.

"You guys are going to Anaheim, aren't you?" The lawyer was on to us.

"Yes, we booked two seats for a flight leaving at six in the morning. You cool?" I asked.

He pondered the situation for dramatic effect. If he got pissed, well, we might have canceled. We might have had an ugly knock-down drag-out if he started flinging things around. With bated breath, we waited.

"Tell you what," he began. "I get it, and I know what it means to you, and yes, there was the out you had with the email, so I can't call B.S. on you. However, I want you to go out with me tonight and ride hard. You can catch your plane in the morning."

"In!" Dave and I shouted in unison.

We didn't know it was part of Bill's plan to change our minds.

Going out with Bill is never a simple night out. You were out, and you were going hard. He took us to this sweet little music joint. There, he fueled our guilt-ridden tummies with tequila. Rounds of shots followed rounds of shots. He was working his plan. After a while, Bill's strategy became apparent. He would get Dave and I passed-out drunk. We would never make a 6:00 a.m. flight at an airport an hour from where we were sleeping. He carried out his plan, and we complied. We got shit-faced. The night was a lot of fun.

We were in a win-win situation. We had a White Sox team with a chance to clinch a pennant, two plane tickets to at least get to the same city as the game, and a backup plan that included sleeping late in the morning and going to see Tom Brady face off against the Jake Plummer-led Denver Broncos.

We were not on to Bill until it was too late. Jose Cuervo had cast his spell. The Roman god Bacchus held us in thrall. We staggered our way back to Bill's house. In the kitchen, he offered us a nightcap. It's a blur whether either of us accepted. We rolled into bed fully clothed. I fortunately remembered to set the alarm for two hours in the future. At 4:00 a.m. the iPhone alarm interrupted us in our twin beds after 120 minutes of restless sleep. I rolled over and looked at Dave.

"We have a decision to make," I said, trying not to lead in which direction I was leaning.

"There is no decision to be made," Dave said as he popped out of bed and went to the bathroom. I did a fist pump from my prone position and gathered my belongings. A few Tylenol, maybe a glass of water, some toothpaste, a quick pee, and we were on our way to DIA. Through a mist of tequila-infused fog, we made it to the airport. I chose the closest parking spot because my new plan was to arrive on Monday morning and change clothes at the airport in time to meet my business guests on Monday. Dave took everything he had. He always travels light. We made our flight, put our tray tables in the locked and upright position, and fell back asleep. Another 120 minutes of shut-eye, and we'd have to be ready.

At 7:30 in the morning local time, we landed at LAX. First pitch was 12 hours away. We didn't have tickets to the game, a hotel, or a rental car. We were most likely wearing sunglasses. I walked down the terminal to who knows where when I realized what part of our plan might present an obstacle.

"Holy shit. We don't have a rental car," I said. Dave was unmoored.

I had a cell phone. Yes, what an invention. I was a Hertz Gold member and had rented overpriced rental cars from Hertz for years. All those rentals were about to pay off. I dialed 1-800-HERTZ Gold. An actual person answered and told me it would be "no problem." A car would be waiting for us when we arrived at the rental facility. It was a small victory on a day when we were hoping for a big one.

When we arrived at the Hertz counter, the neon sign with my name revealed our parking space number. Dave and I glanced around the lot and found our spot. In it was a cherry red Ford Mustang convertible. Of course. High five! Another minor win on a day when we were looking for the biggest win. We started the engine, dropped the top, cranked the radio, and headed out onto Ventura Boulevard. We rubbed our eyes. Dave was in the front seat, and I was driving. It seemed anything was possible. The Sox were running down their dream. We went to Disneyland.

Our plan took shape as we drove. We would go to the ESPN Zone in Disneyland to watch some NFL football starting on the East Coast. The Chicago Bears would kick off soon as well. We could watch the game and be close to Angel Stadium of Anaheim.

At this stage of the season, the Bears were an afterthought. That might have helped them. With the city's attention on the Sox, the highly regarded Bears had a disappointing start to the young season, falling to 1-3. That would change today. We watched an impressive defensive display as the Bears established themselves as a force with a 28-3 thrashing of the Minnesota Vikings at Soldier Field. They would win 10 of the next 12 on their way to a conference championship at 11 and 5. However, this was months into the future. We had a baseball game to get to.

Fully awake by now, we shifted our focus to our next challenge- tickets to the game. Angel Stadium was five miles away. It was a place Dave and I had never been to before. The clock ticked past two in the afternoon in LA. The Broncos were taking the field in Denver. We planned our strategy. Time to get to the ballpark for scalped tickets. We headed over to Anaheim hours before the first pitch. When we arrived, Dave got excited. "They are trying to sell tickets a mile away from the stadium. We will have no trouble getting tickets." Spoken like a true scalper, or is he a scalpee?

Dave had been on both ends of the scalper's wheel for some time. Finding his way into major sporting events and sold-out concerts across the globe. He was ecstatic about the sheer number of tickets available so far from the stadium. He knew we could wait the market out for the best deal. So, we went to a bar.

The little neighborhood surrounding Angel Stadium was enticing. Though not as compact as Wrigleyville in Chicago or the series of neat taverns surrounding Coors Field in Denver or Boston's famed Fenway, Anaheim has game. A series of chic LA sports bars and a congenial environment makes the pre-game here a thrill. Throw in the added atmosphere of an ALCS game moments away, and you have a delightful mix of energy and anticipation. The area would soon be rocking.

Dave and I found an open table, sat back, and admired the Southern California scene. We were playing it cool. Dave insisted we didn't overplay our cards. We had $1000 in cash we could spend on tickets in due time. As we waited the market out, we sat quietly, admiring the tan lines as they walked by. On the TV, we watched the Broncos jump out to a big lead over the Patriots. We were happy for Bill and the hippy friends that he asked to take our place at the game. They, of course, were thrilled. Bill, too, had laughed it all off. We were good on that front.

From time to time, scalpers would make their way to our open-air table and ask if we needed tickets. An extremely persistent seller took a different approach. He asked me where I wanted to sit.

I said, "What?"

He pulled out a ticket seating chart of Angel Stadium and said, "Point where you want tickets, and I'll get them."

This was an experienced entrepreneur offering us made-to-order seats for a price to be determined later. He presented a color-coded map of all the sections inside the park. I preferred two sections. One near the White Sox on-deck circle or one by the Angels. Nothing more than 10 rows off the field. I gave him sections 113 or 123. He told me he'd be right back. After he left, Dave made a reconnaissance trip through the area. He said the Angel fan base has given up, and ticket prices are plummeting. Tickets flooded the market.

A few minutes later, as Brady began picking the Broncos' secondary apart to draw within eight points after falling behind by 25, the scalper returned with section 113 about six rows off the field. I was ecstatic. "How much?!" Notice the exclamation point at the end of my sentence. I was not a skilled negotiator. My unabashed enthusiasm for these great seats for a potential AL pennant-clinching game worked against my best interests.

He answered me calmly, "250 bucks each."

I may or may not have said, "Done." Or, I may have turned to Dave first. All I knew was he had me at $250. Dave said, "What's face value?"

I looked at the tickets in my hand and said, "$125."

Dave said, "That's what we are paying."

He took the air out of my balloon. My enthusiasm waned. I couldn't force a friend to spend an extra $125 he didn't want to pay. I didn't want these tickets to slip away. Fortunately, Dave had calmer nerves and a better plan.

The scalper drew his ire. "Nah, man. These are right where you wanted them," he told me.

As the scalper implicated me, I looked to Dave, then sheepishly spoke, "He is kinda right. They are right where..."

Dave cut me off and turned his attention to the scalper. I was being removed from the bartering because of my overt emotional connection.

"Face value, that's it," Dave pronounced.

The scalper looked disgruntled and stepped back. If he had simply walked away, I would have jumped him from behind and given him $500 for both tickets. I didn't want him to leave with those seats. He didn't go. The number one rule of negotiating is to be prepared to walk away. He didn't. Dave had him.

"Nah, come on, man, $250," he pleaded. He probably would have made a sale if he had said $225 each. Instead, he dug in on his initial offer. Since he had already shown his weakness by not leaving the table, Dave zeroed in. He asked me to hold the tickets and ensure they were where we wanted them. I also inspected them to be sure they were legit and not counterfeit. I gave them the once and twice over. Having the tickets physically in my hand gave the seller the impression that the tickets were no longer his. In my hands now, possession influenced the bargaining. It is nine-tenths of the law, as they say.

Dave said, "I'll tell you what. We will flip you for them."

"Say, what?"

"Flip ya. You know, a coin flip," Dave reiterated.

This crazy-ass turn of events got the attention of others at the restaurant. Though we had entertained ticket sellers since we walked into the place, this encounter had become a little more animated. As the first pitch drew near and we took a hard line on the price, or at least Dave had taken a hard line, the attention of the revelers in the bar moved towards us. The waitress came by and said, "What's going on?"

I said, "Well, we just offered a coin flip to determine how much we should pay for these tickets." I waved the ducats in the air.

"What? That's awesome. I want to flip the coin," the waitress said.

We had him now; Dave set the trap. With a few fellow patrons getting wind of the process and our server stepping up to play referee, there was no way the scalper could resist the gamble. It seemed like every eye in the saloon focused on his response.

"Yea, ok. How does this work?" he asked.

Dave stepped forward and explained. "Simple. If we win the coin flip, we pay you face value. If you win, we pay $250 each."

"Deal."

We had a flipper and a wager, and now we needed a venue. The waitress said let's take this outside. As dozens circled us in the parking lot, the waitress grabbed a quarter and clarified the outcomes. "Ok, if it is tails, they pay $250. If it's face, they pay face." We all got her quick turn of a phrase and nodded our collective heads. That's right. Terms accepted.

I looked around and was stunned at the crowd this little bargaining escapade had drawn. There were now a couple of dozen fans of mixed allegiances looking to see the fate of a $250 coin flip. Heads! Face value. We win. Good sign number three. Another small win on the day when we were searching for the ultimate victory.

We headed into the first pennant-clinching opportunity for the White Sox since September 22, 1959. Two years before my birth. We settled into our perfect seats amidst a crowd of red-clad patrons. We were smack dab in the middle of the Angels' most robust fan base: their premium season ticket holders.

There are two words for this game: Joe Crede. Joe Fucking Crede. Ok, three words. In baseball, you do not expect the number eight hitter in the lineup to be a game-changer. The number nine hitter in the modern American League garners more respect. The eighth hitter is a great fielder with minimal hitting skills. However, in a short playoff series, anyone can change a game, a series, and a season. And when your number eight hitter is Joe Crede, you are destiny bound.

Crede had already hit a walk-off double in Game 2 after the Pierzynski-dropped-third debacle. Now, he stood in the batter's box with nobody on in the seventh. Angels led, 3-2. Then the blow. Crede struck one deep to the left, gone. Game tied. We jumped out of our seats, much to the dismay of the hordes of red and navy partisans around us. We clapped, high-fived, and hollered as we watched Super Joe waltz around the bases. I got the feeling. That blow changed the game, the series, and our Chicago sports-loving lives. There was plenty of baseball left; however, you felt the air in the stadium let out. The home crowd felt defeated.

The Angels' players sunk their heads as Crede jogged the bases. Watch the video on YouTube and take note when Crede rounds third and heads for home. You can barely make out two guys standing six rows up from the on-deck circle, wearing black in a sea of red. It was Dave and I on national TV, cheering deliriously. My heart swelled as Crede finished one of the most memorable home run trots I'll ever witness. Though Crede wasn't finished, the Angels were.

Crede came to bat again in the next inning. This time, with two outs, full count, and Sox runners on first and second. Time for some Ozzie Guillén-style small ball. Crede swats one up the middle. It clears the pitcher's mound. Angels' second baseman Adam Kennedy goes deep into the hole, dives to his right, and nabs it on the outfield grass. There is no way to get Crede at first. He fires home to throw out the Sox's Aaron Rowand, trying to score from second base on a ball that didn't get past the infielders. His throw from his knees is on target, just a tad late. Rowand scores, Sox lead.

Now I digress to the beauty of the game of baseball. This small play typifies the little things in the game. It's a play lost to most in their memory of the Sox's 2005 drive to glory. It is a typical baseball situation taken for granted. However, it speaks volumes about fundamentals. The rudimentary skill of running the bases. The assumption in baseball is with a single, runners advance one base—a double results in a two-base advancement. Now and then, you can 'steal' a base from an opponent on a hit with a heads-up running play. At times, the circumstances dictate you must.

The Sox had runners on first and second as Crede worked the count full with two outs. Since the next pitch would either be the third out, a walk, or a ball put into play, the runners could run as soon as the pitcher released the ball. Rowand took off from second as soon as Angel's reliever, Felix Rodriguez, threw the ball—and he never stopped. The rushed throw home was late because Rowand had that early jump. Baseball. Sox lead, 4-3, in the eighth. Joe Crede. Joe Fucking Crede.

After the Sox took the lead in the eighth, Dave and I began our migration, along with dozens of other Sox fans, to the first base side of the field. We needed to get behind the Sox dugout for the last outs. As we walked up the stairs to the concourse from our third-base seats, we noticed Angel fans leaving. The home crowd had seen enough. We positioned ourselves strategically on the first base concourse as the Sox added a few insurance runs in the ninth. Sox fans clamored all around us. They had the same designs as us. Get as close to the Sox dugout as possible. They, however, were waiting for the game to end. Dave and I didn't. As the final inning progressed, we did as well. After each pitch, we'd poach a different seat. Starting about 20 rows from the field, we were far more focused on the empty seats ahead of us than the action on the field. We had a mission: front row by out 27.

At each pitch, we noticed another couple of seats vacated by the Angels' unfaithful. And with each pitch we'd cunningly advance down the aisle. As hordes of Sox patrons held back in the concourse, we were getting closer to where we wanted to be: in the Champagne seats. Another Angels' fan leaves, which meant another row upgrade for Dave and me. When Casey Kotchman's

easy ground ball ended up in Paul Konerko's mitt for the unas-
sisted putout, Dave and I were pounding the top of the Sox dugout
in elation. Our descent down the aisle had climaxed with the
final out.

The Chicago White Sox punched their ticket to the World
Series. I feel a need to write that beautiful sentence again. The
Chicago White Sox punched their ticket to the World Series. José
Contreras got three easy outs in the ninth to finish one of the more
remarkable stats in post-season history. After the Game 1 loss,
the Sox starters threw four complete games in a row. Contreras,
Buehrle, Freddy Garcia, and Jon Garland, in fact, pitched all but
two outs over the five-games. That's 44-1/3 innings out of 45. The
Angels batted .179 for the series. Remarkable.

The party in planning for 46 years unfolded right in front of
us. It was a moment of pure euphoria, the likes I had never experienced before. The Men in Black had finally done it. We were going
to the World Series. Over the next few hours, I would experience
waves of emotions and thoughts of the generations that had only
imagined this sacred space. It was weird: the sense of kinship I felt.
It was a sensation that spread from my fellow fans in the Anaheim
stands to the ballers on the field to the now-deceased relatives who
followed this team through the ages. I thought of my grandfather,
Pops, who watched thousands of baseball games. He told me about
hearing the air raid sirens that were blared throughout Chicago
when the 1959 White Sox clinched the pennant. He was not much
older than I was now. I strangely thought of firefighters, police-
men, and women who help make the city work. I thought of those
unfortunate fans of the Chicago Cubs whose similar wait just got
a whole hell of a lot longer. That sentiment was welling up inside
me, and tears formed.

The air smelled of spilt beer and jasmine from the palm trees,
but it might as well have been napalm because it was the smell
of victory. Back home, the local TV channels were breaking into
regular programming for the biggest news story in Chicago in

years. Dave and I soaked in the mad excitement. As friends and family hugged at home, they recognized someone on their TV. We were there, front and center in the celebration, and they became even more engaged in the moment's happiness. Later, they would tell me that seeing me at the game heightened their joy. It was that connection thing. It's the thing Ray Kinsella is told by Terrance Mann in Field of Dreams, "The one constant through all the years, Ray, is baseball." This night reminded me of all that was good. It was the purest sense of delight, rivaled only by the birth of a baby.

The team's on-field celebration endured for a lifetime. When it ended, the players acknowledged us as they headed into the locker room. We got hand slaps as they headed into the clubhouse inside the dugout, under where we were standing. When the last player left the field, we, the fans, looked at one another. We were complete strangers in name, but the same in heart. A concert of like souls erupted amongst us.

We celebrated with each other. The night's events commemorated the end of the Yankee dynasty of the 1960s when they owned the American League and finished ahead of the Sox year after year to claim the lone AL playoff spot. On this evening of evenings, the roar of the faithful who journeyed to California on a whim echoed the sound of the South Side Hit Men and the rollicking 1970s when Comiskey Park earned its nickname as the largest outdoor saloon in the world. Our shared joy that evening overcame the 1980s crazy-ass uniforms and the large bodies of Richie Zisk and Greg Luzinski. We basked in the memory of the 1990s and the loaded yet underperforming teams of Frank Thomas, Robin Ventura, Black Jack McDowell, and others who fell victim to the other team of the 1990s: the Cleveland Indians.

We were the fans who endured it all. Here we were, hugging one another, strangers but also Brothers of the Black. Connected to each other by waves of disappointment and near thrills. We looked into each other's eyes and saw all the hurts and the almosts.

The waiting, being the hardest part, was over. Shining through it all this evening was the joy of no longer having to wait. The arrival of Summer. A day when happiness stepped up to greet us. All the good in the world, indeed. We just started hugging and high-fiving each other because the energy demanded it.

A few players returned to the field, and a few threw beers to the fans. The media continued to broadcast live from a few feet in front of us. We were unpaid background extras on this Hollywood set of real life. We represented the Men in Black. The South Side. Dave and I represented that night—and the night was still young. We had a 6:00 a.m. flight back to DIA. The Southern California sun had just set. We had a few hours to kill. The Sox were going to the Ship and invited us to the party.

After a prolonged hour of ebullient feelings, security finally cleared the park. They were the most indulgent of us Sox fans. Here we were, an hour after the game, when security should have been home asleep, and they let us wallow in joy. They patiently stood by us to ensure none of us made a run for the field or did something foolish. They also allowed the party to go on—very California chill. However, as the clock ticked past 11:00 p.m., we needed to leave the park. A group of about 150 turned and looked at each other, "Now what?"

A few started murmuring about the bar across the street. We all said, "Onward." The group moseyed out of the park, through the parking lot and across the street en masse. In the bar, we found more Sox fans bonding and cheering anything and everything. Replays played on the screens above, and we exchanged more high fives. I came across some friends from the neighborhood I did not know were in Anaheim. More hugs, high fives, and shared bliss. The night rolled on until the barkeep called for the last call. It was nearly midnight.

"Last call?! But we just won the pennant! The White Sox are going to the World Series! It's the first call in 46 years!" echoed the patrons as bar management swept us out of the place.

The overworked but well-tipped bartender understood our extreme disposition; however, his license was at stake, and we needed to clear out.

"But to where?"

"Oh, the place down the street is open until four," he politely and encouragingly offered.

So again, en masse, now nearly 200 fans dressed in white and black marched from one bar down the street to the next. Walking in errant lines while bumping into each other, the White Sox faithful would offer each other a high five instead of an "Excuse me." We made it to a bar the size of an airport hangar. It was now Monday morning in SoCal. We were not expecting much. What we discovered was an extravaganza of good feelings and acknowledged joy.

A packed bar, of predominantly Angels fans, awaited us. They seemed celebratory in an "it's a Friday night" way. I thought they were a little overjoyed, to be honest. I soon realized why. Several Angels players had made their way to the bar, where they were blowing off steam and dealing with the anguish of an early elimination from the playoffs. Their fans were celebrating their outstanding season while we were celebrating ours, which would continue in a few days.

We joked, kidded, and shared some conversations with the likes of Jarrod Washburn and Kevin Gregg. They were very respectful of the White Sox and were most cordial, and we reveled for hours in this Angels-fueled Sox-inspired atmosphere. The place was raging until it closed at 4:00 a.m. We had a flight in two hours, and we were hungry. We had a quick stop at Denny's and drove back to the airport. No hotel, no shower, and no way we would forget this evening. The White Sox were on their way to the World Series, and I had a busy day of business calls ahead. Delight overcame me.

I'm sure I snored and smelled the entire flight back to Denver. Apologies to my fellow travelers, who I doubt were White Sox fans. I landed at Denver International Airport about ninety minutes before my associates arrived. A busy day of sales calls and a client dinner were on the agenda. It was 10:00 o'clock in the morning. Jubilation needed to sustain me.

I deplaned and headed toward my car. There I grabbed my suit, tie, shirt and shoes: the uniform of an account executive in 2005. I grabbed my garment bag and Dopp kit and went looking for a shower. Fat chance, but it was one of those details I overlooked in my tequila-fueled planning 30 hours ago. I found an isolated bathroom off the concourse and showered in the sink. Stripped shirtless, I rubbed soapy water into my armpits, dosed my head, and attempted a quick shampoo with squirts from the soap dispenser. I dried off with paper towels—a lot of paper towels. Then I went into a stall for a change of clothes. I hurried as the clock was ticking to show time. Charged with the energy of seeing one of my ultimate sports dreams come true, I was efficient and clean. Well, clean enough.

I returned my Sox garb to the car, grabbed my briefcase, and returned to baggage claim to hook up with my clients. With 15 minutes to spare, I found a wall. With my back against the wall, I slid down it, planted my butt on the ground, and bawled.

I cried with such emotion. The kind of cry that makes you hiccup. It was the complete opposite of grief. I reached what Zen masters try to achieve: complete contentment. An overall cheerfulness overcame me and overwhelmed my ability to control my emotions. I wept—actual tears of unbound euphoria. I still remember the rapture. It spilled out of my eyes, and I covered my mouth as I felt the urge to scream and yell. Hundreds of people were going about their business in this public place. Overcome with glee, I couldn't contain myself. I became a transport of delight. With my years of fandom fully compensated, I felt complete.

The Sox championship felt like love requited. In her memoir, *Lost & Found*, Kathryn Schulz expounds on the difference between longing and searching for love and then finding it. She suggests that most writers of love stories belabor the search for love. Two people looking for each other. The story simply ends happily ever after once they find it. Schulz searches for further meaning in the living of love: the requited part. According to her, living love is "to desire what we already have." That was my feeling on that airport floor in Denver. It's the feeling of "all I ever want is this." Getting it once was enough for me. Everything else would be gravy. I felt I couldn't ask the baseball gods for much more. I had seen what I came to see. Yet, there was so much more.

2nd INNING

Sitting there in the Denver airport like a squonk in my pool of tears, I thought of my older brother, John. He was the epitome of an older brother. Even though I was two years younger, he included me in on his adventures in juvenile delinquency while also ensuring that I didn't get hurt or caught in our shared acts of misbehavior. He'd allow me to ride in the car with his buddies, constantly watching out for me and instructing me in the ways of this hidden world. He did what big brothers were supposed to do: teaching you the things—sex, drugs, and rock and roll—that your parents would not.

My brother was all that. I watched him from the stands with a great sense of pride as he helped lead our high school hockey team to the state championship final. We would take weekend golf trips and he'd always get a ticket for me to see a rock concert together. We also were splitting season tickets to the Chicago Blackhawks. As the years progressed and the Blackhawks went into a dozen-year funk, my personal life was changing as well. My personal situation evolved into husband-hood and then fatherhood, added to the increasing financial pressures and demands of starting my business led to the realization that perhaps the Blackhawk season ticket purchases were not financially savvy nor the best use of my pressed time.

Meanwhile, the White Sox were building a new stadium. The team offered a chance to purchase season tickets for the last year of Comiskey Park with the guaranteed option of buying seats in the new stadium. I took a tour with a season ticket rep, which my son would become some 30 years later. He sat me in these perfect seats. Twenty rows back of visitor's on-deck circle above the net in foul ball heaven and, of course, on the aisle. The net would stop any line drives from smashing your face; however, a few lazy pop-ups may land in your hot dog, which did, in fact, happen. (My son still has that ball with a mustard stain on it.)

The financial commitment was substantial. I would need to create a syndicate of friends to buy. I felt these seats warranted the expense; however, I needed to be financially responsible. I had to drop my Blackhawks' tickets. I told my brother the news. He didn't take it well. He posed a question no sports fan should ever have to answer. It was the King Solomon question of fandom.

"What would you rather see, a White Sox' World Series or a Blackhawks' Stanley Cup winner?"

Posed to you in a bar with a table full of acquaintances, it might appear as nothing more than a conversation starter. A variety of careless answers would lead to more philosophical tangents about individual sports merits or the discussion of franchise worthiness. Someone might say they'd prefer neither and pontificate on their desire to see something like a Bears' Super Bowl win. It would all be a matter of jocular banter on a Saturday night.

However, when John asked me at that moment, it was a dead serious inquiry. It was a blood loyalty question whose answer had magnitude. A defining moment in a relationship along the lines of, "Do you love me?"

I grasped the enormity of the proposition. There would be ramifications for my answer. I pondered it. Deeply. Reflecting on our shared history as hockey players and the idol worship of Blackhawks' players, I thought about the two of us listening to Lloyd Pettit and then Jim West doing the Hawks' play-by-play on

WBBM AM radio. I recalled anxiously awaiting the outcome of a scrum as West bellowed into the microphone, "There's traffic in front of the Hawks' net!" Followed by "Brilliant save by Tony O." I recalled our kitchen floor hockey games while Mom and Dad were out; the basement piano that was used more often as a goal for slap shots than for producing music. With this kind of history, I knew my answer would carry some weight.

I took it all in. I answered, "A Sox World Series."

It took some time for John to get over it. He ignored me for a while. I knew my answer had resonance; however, I expected him to respect my answer. He was unwavering in his disgust. It hurt him badly. It was a wound that took a significant amount of time to heal. I would try a few things to rectify the situation, but it was always there from that point forward. This was the salt I tasted as my tears gushed out of my eyes at the Denver airport. It was my ideal. My soul was revealed. My love of sports requited.

Following that emotional release, my business day became a blur of activity. My associates arrived on time. I greeted them professionally, and off to work we went. A series of sales calls that I had to "be on." I was never one to share my personal life with my staff or my business clients. I tried desperately to keep the two separate. Though I ended up with two terrific friends from my business life, I was mostly at arm's length in sharing my personal escapades. I'd tell them I was married, and my wonderful wife would appear at certain functions. Mostly, I lived separate lives. They did not need to know about my adventures on weekends with friends or the extravagance of my well-earned family vacations. That was my personal business.

That was certainly easier to do in the pre-social media age. Though images of Dave and me in Anaheim appeared on local TV broadcasts at home, there were no viral posts of me floating on the internet for anyone to see. MLB took the only photos that exist from that night. (I couldn't afford the rights to have them appear in this memoir).

That day in the Mile-High City, I didn't share the thrill I had experienced in the last 24 hours with anyone on this business day. As my personal energy tank was running empty, I had to come clean with my employee. I told him I was running on fumes and had not slept but for maybe 20 minutes on the flight from LA. He was stunned at how well I had been performing. It was a unique strength of mine, no doubt. I could run with the dogs at night and fly with the eagles in the morning. It was one of my gifts, which paved the way for business success. Being able to hang with certain clients into the wee hours of the night, answer the early morning alarm bell, and deal with other clients who were 'morning people' made me a sensation. I don't get hangovers. Whenever someone asks "How does he do it?" you know you are succeeding. Keep them in awe. It helps to know your limitations as well.

I was treading water throughout the day, and we still had a major client dinner coming up, which required a masterful performance from me. On top of this, I was fielding phone calls from friends and family who saw me on TV the night before. They told me about their celebrations at home. Seeing me there heightened their excitement. They wanted me to know they were there with me in spirit. We shared a communal feeling that sports and their tribal nature elicited.

I was utterly exhausted. My staffer needed to cover for me and back me up. He did, and I slept for an hour. Then I was off to the client's dinner. It was one of those Fogo de Chão places where they bring large chunks of meat to your table, slice it, and drop it off. Moments later, more food shows up at the table to be devoured. It was a Roman feast. I looked at it as the AL pennant celebration. Envisioning the White Sox players enjoying a similar banquet, I felt like Caesar. Sure, I was paying for this monster meal for a dozen clients, yet it felt warranted. I was reaping the bounty of a trip to the World Series professionally and personally. My team had made it. My business had achieved success. I was the king, enjoying the spoils. The smell of braised lamb chops and horseradish sauce was the scent of a winner. I had come into my own.

The next day, things returned to normal. I made some sales calls and eventually boarded a plane to Chicago. Back home, I couldn't avoid the thrill. People stopped me on the street to say they saw me on TV. As they shared their excitement, I realized I was their surrogate and seeing me there made them feel even closer to the moment. The return to my office was like a conquering hero returning from battle. My staff regaled in the joy. I stopped in to see my mom and dad, who still lived in my childhood home. We shared hugs and a censored story of my past 48 hours. They too had seen me on TV. The night continued to resonate. Delight surrounded me.

3rd INNING

In 1995, when my dad was 66, a few years older than I am now, he sat down to write his autobiography. He penned it in his impeccable handwriting on a yellow legal pad - his notebook of choice for his entire life. He called his short manuscript, "The Story of My Life."

His family's financial circumstances forced my dad to forego many of the simple pleasures of being a child. His father struggled to stay employed and with six children, the situation often demanded they move in with relatives. These frequent moves kept the family unit a revolving door of acquaintances and experiences. While living with extended family in his grandmother's house, he witnessed his abusive uncle threatening my dad's mother with a knife. Time to move on.

Most of their residencies were on Chicago's far southwest side, near Midway Airport. My dad never seemed to be too far from a rail yard. In his unpublished life story, he details his typical day during his high school years while attending Tilden Tech - a

Chicago public school. He took a job working overnights in the train shipping yard to help the family with the bills. His primary task was to wake engineers who were sleeping in their cabooses when it was time for their train to depart. He eventually honed his skills as a father who had an uncanny way of waking us up for school. It usually mounted to a solid hand clap and a repeated sing song mantra. "Time to get up. Time for school." We rarely slept in at home.

His typical day as a teenager had him taking a streetcar to school five miles away. After school, the streetcar would get him home by 3:00pm. After homework and chores, he'd sleep till 10:30pm. Upon waking, it would be a mile walk to his job where he'd put in an eight-hour shift from 11:00pm till 7:00am. Then he'd catch the streetcar again to school by 8:00am.

This left my father with no time to play. It hurt him deeply. He writes, "I guess I wasn't supposed to have fun. That was for my friends. I shall never forget the afternoons stepping off the streetcar at 69th and State, walking thru the prairie, seeing my friends playing baseball or football wishing I could join them. But I couldn't. Because their playtime was my sleep time, to rest for another day at work that began at 11:00pm."

His work ethic paid off in his twenties. His steady employment allowed him to purchase a car - a real luxury in 1949. This fortuitous purchase led to the young Johnny being asked on a blind date as a wingman for Wally Clifford. Clifford needed a ride. On that fateful day, my dad pulled up to the Walgreens at 63rd and Western Ave in Chicago and met a 17-year-old named Joan Sloup. Fifty years after that meeting, my dad wrote in his memoir, "I can still envision that skinny little brunette walking across Western Avenue wearing a grey coat that seemed to flow down to her ankles. She had bangs. She was cute. She was fun." She'd soon be his wife.

Three months after he married my mother in October 1950, the US Army drafted my father to serve in Korea. Though my dad had only a high school education (a graduate of the College of Hard Knocks he would continually remind us), they promoted him to radio operator. He attributed his promotion to radio communications man as a factor of his high IQ. His aptitude kept him off the front lines. According to his journal, his unit was part of the fastest advance and fastest retreat on the Korean battlefield. As he wrote in the unpublished autobiography, "Many of the guys I came over with were sent to the front lines and many of them lost their lives."

When he returned from his nineteen month tour of duty, my mother was waiting for him. He called it one of his life's "Golden Moments." He would share many of those through the years, including the birth of his firstborn, my sister, Kathy (Blakemore). After Kathy's birth on January 9, 1955, my mother experienced a series of miscarriages. Family lore is uncertain; however, it's possible my mother suffered nearly a dozen total miscarriages over her child-bearing years. In the interim after my sister's birth, my parents took in foster children. They named one of them, Richard Louis. Rick ended up staying a lifetime, as my parents adopted him shortly after his arrival in their home.

That apparently opened the floodgates. Starting on New Year's Eve 1959, my mother had three boys in quick succession, starting with my brother John, followed by me 16 months later and then my little brother Dan in January 1963. A few more miscarriages followed before the family rounded out with David Scott in 1968 and the "practice grandchild," my baby brother Chris, born in July 1970. The seventh child of the family who made front page news in the *Chicago Tribune* when he turned 7 on 7/7/77.

My dad made sure the early lives of my five brothers and sister were not similar to his. He started a business with a couple of co-workers who eventually left my dad as the sole owner of Dober Chemical (now The Dober Group) in 1957. Ten years later, we moved from a quaint community in Oak Forest, Illinois where my parents helped start the Catholic parish of St. Damian, to the home we would know for forty years in the tiny suburb of

Flossmoor. There, our home life was one part *Wonder Years* and one part *Wayne's World*. In his memoir *Sting-Ray Afternoons*, Steve Rushin shares stories of growing up in a neighborhood similar to my personal experience. He describes it as "where life was never more lively."

My dad loved baseball or the idea of us playing baseball, which is what has resonated through the generations of Dobrezes. My dad saw the game as a metaphor for life. On the diamond, he used the travails of the game to teach important lessons we could translate to our future selves. One of his most vital mottos is now etched on a stone monument in his memory at our hometown little league ballpark in Flossmoor, Illinois.

"You can't hit the ball unless you swing the bat."

Like the tablet handed down by Moses himself, every offspring of my dad knows the verse. It acts as a guiding principle for any sports endeavor or life pursuit. For me, it became my North Star, a beacon of promise. A pledge to myself. If I see a chance, I'll take it.

My dad's approach to coaching youth baseball was fascinating. Nowadays, a parent's coaching route is to follow their child through the ranks. As they progress to each age, they shadow the child thru to the high school level. Some continue on as far as they can milk the association. My dad was different. He stayed put in the rookie league. He never left the eight- and nine-year-olds and thus could coach all of us boys as we aged through the league. Regardless of talent or potential, my dad coached each of us (boys) for two years in the introduction league. We all cherished those seasons. We were not alone in our appreciation of those lessons learned on the diamond.

At my dad's funeral in 2010, dozens of men mentioned my dad's influence on them in rookie league baseball at Flossmoor. They knew him as Mr. Gopher. The league had this fascinating concept of naming teams in each league after a different sports conference. The Rookie League, as it was called, mimicked the Big Ten Conference. Teams named the Spartans, Wolverines, and

Badgers battled the Gophers on the dirt infields just off Western Avenue School. Once you finished your two-year stint in the Rookies, you advanced to Triple-A, where you became hockey teams (Blackhawks, Maple Leafs, Red Wings, etc.). It was only in your fifth year in the program when you finally made the Majors (now referred to as Bronco) and had the chance to wear the logo and colors of MLB teams. After those two years, you advanced to Pony, and you'd play on your favorite football team. It was the only time I enjoyed being a Packer!

The men remembering my dad at his services spoke of the influence and power of his guidance when they were at an impressionable young age. One of them said to me, "It's weird, it was over 50 years ago, however, I still remember the impression he made on me." His spirit, as Mr. Gopher, was of a man in full. He understood where we were in our current development and used the game to give us instructions on life. He molded our character. A benevolent dictator in business, however, on the baseball diamond, he was a teacher—a mentor to young, developing minds.

Recently, I spent a weekend with a friend in Utah. During my stay, he pulled out a keepsake to show me. It was a 1970 League Champions trophy from our nine-year-old baseball team. It was a trophy he won as a Gopher, being coached by my dad. He had held on to it through numerous moves to many cities. And here it was, all six inches of golden glory. A statue of a batter heading to first base mounted on a piece of marble no bigger than a deck of cards. It was fifty-three years old. He told me it was the only trophy he ever kept. I viewed it as a silent tribute to my dad.

My dad saw each practice and game as an opportunity to corral our spirits and keep us present. He encouraged risk to stand out and achieve. Just give it a try was his mantra. He didn't coach any other sports or any other age group. Yet, he significantly impacted not just his children over those two years under his guidance, but dozens of other future men of our community over his 10-year reign as Mr. Gopher.

Perhaps the most significant gesture was that of the anonymous donor who paid for and installed that monument to my dad that rests forever at our village's ball field. My family is still unaware of the kind individual who thought enough of my father's influence to lay a marker to his years as Mr. Gopher. It sits peacefully like him, under an American flag.

For my kids, it was different. I followed them through their multi-year development in various sports, from basketball and softball to field hockey camps and long snapper clinics. I was trying to keep them engaged and had an undue influence on what they did. I became the baseball league president, and with that came hours at the ballpark before and after games each night. As a father, I had responsibilities to be with them and around them, so if I was at the fields, they were at the fields. Softball became the center of my young girls' lives. Maybe it was not the best thing, but it became our thing. It was what we did. We fostered community and friendships at the park.

We met a group of parents and children from the same age bracket who became fast friends. Together, we traversed the years of child-rearing, puberty challenges, and the risk of bad influences in their lives. We tried to build a safe environment for our children to grow, but we also had vices ourselves. We wanted to win and were driven by an odd sense of personal worth wrapped up in our child's prowess on the field. In retrospect, that mindset sounds crazy. It seemed like much of our self-worth was contingent on the results on the diamond. We couldn't bear losing. The kids seemed to handle things much better than we did.

We got a little too caught up in it. Youth sports provide opportunities to learn and form bonds. Being part of a team proved crucial to my children's overall development, particularly for my young girls. I wish I had handled it a little better. I'm going to give myself a B-minus. In terms of overall presence and involvement, I was an A+. I organized leagues, drove my kids to distant locations, and paid for things endlessly. I also suffered from being vicarious.

Possessed by a certain hopefulness that they would excel, their accomplishments became a badge of honor for me to wear around town. Simultaneously, it was about spending time with them. I didn't want their youth to be an emptiness of them explaining to everyone where their dad was. I was present with a concerted attempt at not being too overbearing.

Parents often make a selfish decision to cultivate their children's interest in a self-satisfying genre. Take the Williams sisters of tennis. As pointed out in the fascinating movie *King Richard*, the father of Venus and Serena, was laser-focused on turning his two girls into tennis superstars. It was a far-fetched idea: two Black girls from Compton rising up in the most country club of sports to become its eventual champions? Outrageous. Yet, Richard Williams saw it and then painstakingly, often at the risk of his own physical harm, persisted. The problem with Richard Williams's story is, it worked.

Parents see Richard's success and then strive to duplicate it. Everyone is in search of Bobby Fischer. Each child has inherent skills, yet parents believe they can develop them because they had a highlight or two of blazing glory back in the day.

Parent over-involvement in children's sports appears to be a recent phenomenon. My mother, for instance, never played a down, inning, quarter, or period of any sport, nor did my sister. In fact, short of a visit to a Chicago Bears' game in her 70s with the entire family, I am challenged to remember another professional game she ever attended. My dad, however, took us to everything, yet we know little of his on-field escapades. He played softball in the local adult league with my uncle post-high school, but we know little about his on-field play.

I tried to fall somewhere in between fanatic and involved. I purposefully designed my business to allow me to be present. Upon release of the season's schedule, I'd jockey my business calendar around my kid's games. When a business opportunity presented itself, I would measure them in terms of time sucked more than money made. Would a new business commitment still allow me to watch a Tuesday night fifth-grade basketball game? I knew it would bring me more cash, and I was confident I could do the job. But I didn't want to be absent. You had to strike a balance.

I coached everything my kids did until they reached high school. After that, I coached a little in high school. I never coached hockey. My kids did not play hockey, and now my son regrets that. Softball, baseball, basketball, and field hockey. My children, bless their hearts, indulged me, and they excelled. As youths, they were standouts. They were solid players who knew the game inside and out. My girls taught me more about friendship, belonging, and relationships than about the game. My son instilled in me the value of grit. I hope I taught them something as well.

They also taught me a fascinating distinction between boys and girls. Boys want to be the king of the mountain, while girls seek to fit in. I realize I am entering some potentially dangerous territory here and wish to explain. I am not by any means categorizing all people into these gender stereotypes. I raised my children the same way, regardless of their gender. If they asked about a sport, hobby, or fashion trend, I encouraged them to pursue it. Regarding sports, the girls showed much more 'teamman-ship' than the boys.

The difference manifested itself in an epic 2005 season when I managed my middle child, Buddy's softball team. She had exhibited a considerable talent for the sport and had played travel ball with the other standouts in our community. Those games challenged her enough. She also took part in the in-house program, which included all the girls in the neighborhood chosen by the various managers to be on specific teams. This selection process was the draft. One season, going into the draft, she gave me explicit instructions to pick her friends first, regardless of talent.

Though it was standard practice to choose the best player on the board for your team, she suggested I downgrade specific selections to ensure that her pals were on the squad. She stated that having them on the team was more important than winning the league championship. Dumfounded, I paid her heed. In various draft rounds, I took players of lesser skills to ensure I stacked the team with her friends. I braced myself for a year of defeats.

However, something miraculous happened. We won almost every game. Playing as a unit, the girls constantly picked each other up. They cheered for every minor increment of improvement of a teammate. Each girl remained focused and exhorted her best effort, not on behalf of themselves or the game's outcome, but in honor of her friends. They didn't want to let each other down. It was a remarkable outcome that fascinates me to this day. A less-than-ideal mix of talent becomes a juggernaut. The other coaches in the draft thought I was nuts until it worked.

The season taught me an interesting lesson. Girls get strength from each other, while boys play alpha games. As a manager, you need to accept and work with each of them to their strengths. The USA women's soccer team exhibits this truth on the national level. As a unit, they bounded together to seek comparable pay to the men's Olympic teams. Even though the ladies had been significantly more successful, the men garnered larger paychecks. The women planted a flag together and negotiated as a unit with the governing bodies. The result was a major turnaround in policy. Can you imagine men exhibiting such unity in contract negotiations? Usually, you will find them harboring for their individual pay.

My daughter's team of friends also brought out my dark side. After that team lost the season opener, they ran off 17 wins in a row to reach the Championship of the in-house league. They were unstoppable. We entered the finals as the odds-on favorite. We lost the game, and I lost my cool. As much as I had prided myself on my calm demeanor in the dugout, I failed that day. I was an embarrassment. After a string of close calls that didn't go our way, the teenage umpire ruled against us one more time. I said some regrettable things to him. He tossed me from the game. It was only a momentary lapse, but it still stings.

I doubt many people remember my ejection, or the fact that we even played this game at all. To me, it remains an unfortunate moment in my maturation process of becoming like my dad: A Man in Full. Concern over the game's outcome overcame me. My ego took control and ran amok. Today, I could not care less about the second-place finish, but my errant behavior continues to haunt me.

4th INNING

With that embarrassment a few months in my rearview mirror, my focus turned to Houston. The Astros had pulled off a significant turnaround in their 2005 season to reach the World Series. After losing 30 of their first 45 games, they clawed their way into a wild card spot after fishing 11 games behind the division leader. (For the record, the Astros were a National League team playing in the NL Central. Their eventual move to the American League was still eight years away). The Astros knocked off the Atlanta Braves in the NLDS and then beat the heavily favored St. Louis Cardinals in the NLCS. Led by the Killer Bs, Jeff Bagwell and Craig Biggio, the Astros had a ticket to the show.

For Bagwell and Biggio, I had nothing but respect. Though I was about to cheer wildly against them, deep inside, I feared their bats heading into the World Series. The two players spent their entire careers with the Astros and played 4,714 games together before the World Series. That, my friends, is not a misprint. A combined 29 seasons before getting to the dance. For Bagwell, this series would mark his last games. With Gold Gloves, All-Star appearances, and Rookie of the Year Awards—the two legends were waiting for the White Sox.

My brothers arranged a conference call. We were all frequent business travelers and spent good portions of each work week on the road. We did our best to clear our schedules before the playoffs. However, recent history had dictated that planning your life around the potential of a Chicago team making the World Series was usually pointless. The six of us, my brother-in-law Blake included, reviewed our current commitments. We had the home games covered and were looking to convene on the road. We decided to meet in Houston for Game 5. Each of us took on a role: booking the hotel, getting tickets, renting a car, and arranging dinner. We all settled on the plan. First, the teams had to play Games 1, 2, 3, and 4.

Nothing clogs the streets like a World Series game. We had attended big games for the White Sox before. The Cubs-Sox games are all sell outs. The previous playoff rounds of this magical 2005 season had their challenges of overflow traffic and tight parking. At the infamous Disco Demolition night, the Sox turned away a reported 10,000 teenagers for the scheduled (emphasis on scheduled) doubleheader against the Tigers. Game 1 of the White Sox - Houston Astros Fall Classic would be far more significant, as thousands showed up without tickets simply to partake in the atmosphere. Ticketed fans, scalpers, hangers-on, and partiers gathered to take in the rarified air of a World Series game in the city of second-place finishes. There was no way to connect with anyone you might have prearranged to meet.

My tailgate plans blew up. The plan called for me to secure the parking spot while others brought the food and drinks. My trustworthy friend Phil Milord had steak duty while my brother, Dan promised the beer. I arrived early and set up in a prime location hours before the first pitch. Then, disaster struck. No one else could get anywhere close to us. Thousands of cars and some ill-prepared traffic directors created a scene outside the stadium of pure chaos. Nobody could get to anyone. Cell phone usage taxed the system, causing poor connections. Folks couldn't get from one point to another. With a cooler full of steaks, Phil had to park nearly a mile away. Brother Dan and the beer were just as far. I showed my rookie status as a World Series tailgate planner. We were stuck with a bag of chips and soda pop. The first World Series game in my lifetime was not off to a good start.

Havoc ruled the day, and I appeared to be unprepared. My guests were livid. They have forbidden me from planning another tailgate for any sport! This became a badge of honor I wore proudly, as all future tailgates only required my presence. They did not trust me to be in charge again. Be it Bears, Sox, or Northwestern football. I simply needed to show up. That was a pleasant treat. However, this game of games was a full-out disaster. We were peasants amongst the lavish spreads of tailgate heaven. An array of meal and drink options surrounded us as we shared a bag of Jay's potato chips. They were, like me, ruffled. Phil eventually arrived with monster steaks that were bigger than my miniature grill. Top that off with the grill tools forgotten at home and you had a laughable disaster.

Hopefully, the Sox would be better prepared. We had an added sense of confidence with us as we caught a break a few days earlier. St. Louis Cardinals' Albert Pujols homered in the ninth inning of Game 5 of the National League Championship Series to push the Houston Astros to a series-clinching Game 6. That victory was a significant benefit to the White Sox. The 'Strohs needed to start their ace, Roy Oswalt, in Game 6, pushing him back in the rotation for the World Series. Our draw for Game 1 of the World Series was an aging and injured Roger Clemens. Believe!

Jermaine Dye lit up the South Side skies with a first-inning home run that electrified the joint. We never came down. It turned out to be just the first blow in a raucous Game 1. A back-and-forth second inning saw the Sox take a 3-1 lead only to watch it disappear in the third. The promised pitching duel appeared to be getting out of hand. The Sox had already dismissed Roger Clemens, and our starter, Jose Contreras, looked vulnerable. With the score deadlocked at 3-3, Joe Crede stepped to the plate. Gone. Sox take the lead, never to relinquish.

Sox manager Ozzie Guillén enhanced the thrill when he walked to the mound in the ninth and gestured with his arms outstretched wide in a chunking motion. "Bring in the big guy," he mouthed as rookie Bobby Jenks entered the game for his first of four straight appearances. He shut down the Astros, and the Sox owned the night and took a 1-0 series lead. Tailgate troubles be dammed; we were up a game in the World Series. It was a night that felt like nothing more in sports could matter.

Like the Jimmy Fallon movie, the town had become fever-pitched for Game 2. Fever Pitch. There is no better way to describe the atmosphere throughout the city and suburbs of Chicago after Game 1. The dramatic victory awoke even the most skeptical to believe. Everywhere you went, the air felt charged. The streets became a kaleidoscope of three colors: silver, white, and black. Flags hanging from houses, pennants were breezing out of car windows, and kids dressed in t-shirts, sweatshirts, and hoodies—all with a singular allegiance. The department stores had rearranged their floor plans overnight. Every store you entered, whether a 7-11 or the fanciest of stores on Michigan Avenue, became stocked with Sox merchandise. It was a magnification of all that is capitalism. Overnight, vast inventories of clothing, posters, banners, and memorabilia appeared on a grand scale. Individual stores overturned their floor plans and put the recently created product front and center. Everyone who was even casually entering these locations had to witness the painting of the town in silver and black.

Sox's success dominated the TV and radio conversation. Bars were suddenly full of expert commentators discussing Buehrle's control and how they knew Scott Podsednik would hit his first home run in the playoffs. They trusted Ozzie Guillén even if they didn't understand a word he said. Our little universe had coalesced around a team, and everywhere you moved in the city and suburbs, you saw the old English font emblem of the Southside's baseball team. The Second City had finally turned into a Sox town.

Game 2 featured two of the game's best on the mound. We had Mark Buehrle going while the Astros were starting Andy Petite. Pettitte would win over 250 games in a Hall-of-Fame caliber career. Years earlier, I watched Pettitte start a game with his parents seated right behind me. I chatted at length with his dad, but it grew increasingly uncomfortable as his son was getting shell-shocked on the mound that day. I was once a parent of a pitcher. My daughter, Becca, pitched in travel softball. When she was on the mound, I felt an unusual tension in my body. As a father or mother of the pitcher, it is nerve-racking. Every pitch has you holding your breath. You were not so afraid of getting hit. You just couldn't stand the walks. In a small way, I could understand what Mr. Pettitte must have been going through. Yet, he was at ease on this high heat index day as his son lasted less than four innings in a White Sox blowout. He stayed until the very end. I respected that. A much more seasoned Pettitte returned to the same park under slightly cooler temperatures—roughly 50 degrees cooler.

The purported pitchers' duel unraveled early as both teams found their bats. The Astros jumped out to a 4-2 lead after five innings. Buehrle found some rhythm and closed down the 'Strohs in innings six and seven, though left trailing by two. As the fans stood to stretch and sing about peanuts and Cracker Jack, the Sox' captain had the best surprise waiting in the batter's box.

Dan Wheeler took the mound and got Joe Crede to pop out before allowing a one-out double to Juan Uribe. Tadahito Iguchi followed a Scott Podsednik strikeout to put two runners on with two outs. Wheeler beaned Jermaine Dye, loading the bases and forcing a pitcher change. Chad Qualls, oh how we love you, stepped on the mound to face Number 14: Paul Konerko. The first pitch Qualls threw made up for a lifetime of longing. The TV call by Joe Buck was simple, "He rips one into left. Konerko. Grand Slam." Then a moment later, "Bedlam in Chicago!"

That's what I heard while jumping up and down with family and thousands of Chicagoans across the metropolitan area in living rooms and bars. It was the shot heard around the 312. It still brings chills. There are moments when the greats exceed expectations and step up to the moment. The list of Sox' great first basemen is long and impressive. From the least appreciated Zeke Bonura (look him up) to Dick Allen and the indomitable Jose Abreu, the Sox have had some legends playing the bag. When the conversation turns to 'the best,' it boils down to Frank Thomas, Konerko, or Abreu. Thomas ranks above all statistically with his Hall-of-Fame career, while Abreu impresses with his consistency during the regular season. Neither Abreu nor Thomas delivered the way Konerko did in the playoffs. His Slam gives him the edge. When needed the most, he stepped up to the plate, and bedlam reigned.

E. Jason Wambsgans, a Pulitzer Prize winning photographer, caught the chaos for posterity. He trained his camera not on the field but on a section of fans along the first baseline. His lens caught my brother Dan. His talented eye captured Dan's delight at the smack of the bat. *The Chicago Tribune* chose the classic shot as a photo of the year. It also appeared in a few glossy magazines that media organizations rush out after a championship season. The photo captured ecstasy.

Konerko's shot holds an extraordinary place in the collective sports memories of Chicagoans because the Sox hung on for the win. It wasn't easy, though. The Sox went to the rookie Jenks again in the ninth, and he pitched tentatively. The Astros rallied for two in the top of the ninth to tie. In the last stanza, it was up to the bottom half of the Sox lineup to face the NL's top closer, Brad Lidge. With one out, 'Scottie Pods' came to the plate. Scott Podsednik had been the major league's stolen base leader for the Milwaukee Brewers in 2004. In his first year with the Sox, he led the league in times caught stealing. However, we never cared. He brought an element to Guillén's small ball the Sox had lacked. He made the 2005 All-Star team. After a dismal performance in the ALDS against Boston, Number 22 found his playoff legs, stealing six bases over 12 games. We knew he was fast. We didn't know he had a superpower.

We would have a serious threat if he could get on base. He drew the hitter's favored count of 2-1. The next pitch was hard to believe, but it made believers out of all of us. Podsednik's first homer of the season (regular or playoffs) was the 14th walk-off homer in World Series history. It was a middle coast version of Kirk Gibson's "I can't believe what I just saw" shot. The team who advised us never to stop believing never stopped surprising us. Any ounce of cheer left after Konerko's slam oozed out of each of us like the last bit of ketchup squeezed out of a bottle. It was exhaustive, yet most rewarding. The Sox had a two-games to-none lead.

Time for a shift of venues. The Sox traveled to Houston as I headed for New York. The demands of business were getting in the way. White Sox baseball consumed me for the past two weeks. It was not just the games themselves but also the constant change of travel plans, the last-minute ticketing to Los Angeles, and the arranging of poorly managed tailgates. It was all-consuming, and I was just a fan. Imagining the players and their focused intensity through this multi-week sprint was mind-numbing.

My professional life, if not on hold, was on an inevitable delay. I was getting the basics done. It was unlikely that I was pushing anything forward. I was treading water at work by design. This is the benefit of running your own business. Perhaps the most significant advantage. Setting aside the agonies of managing people and stressing over monthly bills, running a business is the best way to go through life. It provides freedom of control. Control over your time. At times, though, it appears to be the opposite. Running a business can put stressors on your timetable like nothing else. Burning the midnight oil and making 6:00 a.m. plane departures is non-stop. Juggling the plates in the air is difficult under normal business pressures. Doing so during a playoff run adds an extra layer of challenge and difficulty—in the same way riding a roller coaster blind can be thrilling.

Business obligations demanded I travel to New York for some forgotten reason on the day the Sox had to play Game 3 in

Houston. I booked my return flight in time to catch the game on TV with the family that night. In the worst-case scenario, I'd miss an inning, but I would likely be in my car driving home, listening to the game on the radio. Something even worse than the worst-case scenario happened.

The airline canceled my flight to Chicago. I found this out at the gate moments before the scheduled take-off. The only solace came from the fact that it was the airline's fault. They would compensate me with a free hotel room and dinner that night near LaGuardia and rebooked me on the first flight out the next day at 6:00 a.m. I hopped on a shuttle bus to the hotel and made the requisite calls home. Resolved to watch the game alone, I wondered whether I might meet some other stranded Chicagoans in the bar tonight and revel with them.

Nestled in my room, I knocked out some business responsibilities and walked down to the lobby bar and restaurant for my free meal and some companionship with like-minded strangers—no such luck. The bar was completely devoid of people of any fandom. I was stunned. Where were they? I finished my meal alone and self-conscious, as a traveling salesperson frequently does. I double-checked my flight reservations to Houston in two days and lounged on the made bed back in my room to watch the game. The Astros had taken a 3-0 lead, and it appeared the night belonged to them. Roy Oswalt had been solid through four innings as the Astros' lead grew to four.

Then came the fifth. Joe Crede hit an Oswalt pitch over the wall, and there was life. Sox trailed 4-1. An Uribe single-held promise. Then the National League's no-designated-hitter rule plagued us. Our pitcher, Jon Garland, struck out in his second at-bat of the season. One down, one on, and a lot of fun to come. Three singles in a row scored two more, cutting the Astros lead to 4-3. I had renewed interest in this one. After a Konerko pop-up, it was A. J. Time. Pierzynski's double scored two more, giving the Sox the lead and a five-run Firth of a Fifth.

After all those fireworks for the visitors, things settled down again for the next three innings. With the Sox ahead 5-4, the Astros drew two walks in the eighth after two outs. Nerves. Remember what I said about walks? The bane of existence for pitchers or their partisan fans. A Jason Lane double tied the score, but the follow-up runner held up at third. A fatal mistake by the Astros' third-base coach? For this scenario, they had inserted Eric Bruntlett as a pinch runner for Mike Lamb. To take the extra base. To challenge the White Sox outfielders, who possessed average arms. Right fielder Podsednik held Bruntlett on third with two outs. A costly running error indeed for the hometown squad. The Sox Dustin Hermanson put an end to the Astros' rally.

We entered the ninth. The Sox moved Konerko along to second base after being hit by a pitch, but left him stranded. The Astros had even more prospects of winning it in their half of the ninth. Orlando Hernandez, a fireballer known for his seesaw performances, lived up to his reputation. This inning was a microcosm of his stint with the White Sox. He had the skill of putting runners on but not letting them score, bending but not breaking. After a walk to Chris Burke, Hernandez had his pinch runner dead to rights on a pick-off play, except he sailed the ball over Konerko at first and the runner moved to second. The runner, Chris Burke, subsequently stole third base and was ninety feet away from scoring the winning run. With one out, any contact would seal the game for the home team. Hernandez amped it up one more time. He book ended strikeouts around an intentional walk and snuffed the rally.

The game headed for midnight and beyond. Being the playoffs with added commercials and the usual manager stalls, this game encroached on my sleep time. There was an early morning flight approaching. I was ratcheting up my intensity; I was not wearing sunglasses. This back-and-forth game was becoming more than pivotal. This was becoming the defining game of the 2005 World Series. I sensed the urgency. I called my brothers all over the country. As the game entered the tenth, I suggested they may need to consider a change of plans. They needed to investigate getting to Houston a day earlier than we had planned. We needed a contingency. I also told them that, hopefully, mom was wrong when she said, "Nothing good ever happens after midnight."

Things were a tad quiet for the first few extra innings. The Sox threatened in the 11th, but that was about it. The hours ticked away. It passed 2:00 a.m. in New York. It was now the longest game in World Series history as it entered the 14th. For the Astros fans, it was looking a bit like déjà vu. They had beaten the Braves a few short days ago in 18 innings. They were up against it again, trying to stay alive in the best of seven.

World Series MVP Jermaine Dye got the inning started with a single, but the Astros quickly erased him with a double play. With two outs, the Sox were deep into their bench. Up to the plate stepped Geoff Blum. Blum was the most average ballplayer you could ever draw up. Over 13 years, he played for eight teams. His career batting average is a dead-perfect measure of mediocrity .250. He was one home run shy of a career 100, but he hit one that got him a bronze statue. Blum's two-out blast off Ezequiel Astacio rocked the South Side of Chicago and the seventh-floor hotel room in Queens. I jumped up and down on my hotel room bed, yelling in complete delirium. I didn't care that it was two in the morning, and I had a flight home in less than four hours. We had the lead.

Something good did not happen after midnight. Something great did. I operated the phones again. I called every one of my brothers and told them point blank, "There will be no Game 5. You must get to Houston tomorrow, or I mean today," since Tuesday had now become Wednesday. The Sox had a shot at winning the World Series in less than 17 hours. Only one answered the call. Well, they all answered the actual phone call, but only one could rearrange his plans to get to Houston in a matter of hours.

I spent the post-game reserving two tickets to paradise or at least to Houston from Chicago. One for me and one for the lone brother to make it, Dan. I caught my 6:00 a.m. flight in a trance of giddiness and rushed home. I again made the "puppy eyes look" at the world's most understanding wife, who said, "Be safe and bring home a winner." I had time for a kiss and maybe lunch and a shower since I neglected that in New York. Again, apologies to my fellow travelers. I grabbed a backpack and drove back to Midway Airport, the same place I had just left two hours ago.

Dan and I left Chicago in the early afternoon. In the pre-Uber era, we needed a car. Despite failed attempts to reserve one with many companies, Dan relied on his super-duper fantastic status with Avis. His level of service included a benefit that granted him a car, no matter what. With every car in the city accounted for, he secured one. Another W for the visitors!

It was less than two hours before game time, so we headed toward Minute Maid Park. We still had no hotel or game tickets. The usual pre-game hubbub greeted us, including a few guys after us with tickets for sale. We spent some time getting the lay of the land and an idea of where we wanted to be and how much we will pay.

We agreed on a face value price for the first base side about 20 rows back—decent seats in a brand-new stadium. Built five years earlier, Minute Maid Park originally was Enron Field. That didn't go over too well. The team was supposed to get over $100 million for the rights over the length of the contract; however, after the first season, Enron went bankrupt in a vast financial scandal. The Astros wanted out of the agreement. Somehow, it worked out that the Astros paid Enron to get out of the deal. Nobody ever accused Enron of having poor lawyers. It became Astros' Field before Minute Maid purchased the naming rights and the 'Juice Box' was christened.

It was a right-handed hitter's paradise with a short porch in left, an awkward wall configuration, and a hill in centerfield with a flagpole in play. A lot of effort went into trying to recreate the magic of ballparks past. Here, the designers were overzealous in

THE WHITE SOX   51

their nostalgia. It was more of a discombobulation. It has since gone through a renovation. Oh, well, "A" for effort.

The fourth game was an edge-of-the-seat pitchers' duel for the ages. The Sox started Freddy Garcia, and the Astros countered with Brandon Backe. Two of the regular season's most consistent starters were set to battle. Both pitchers bent but rarely broke. Such was the case in the early going as a Sox triple in the third went to waste. A few innings later, another rally produced no runs.

As Dan and I contemplated finding a hotel to stay overnight for tomorrow's Game 5, Astros manager Phil Garner blinked. He went to "Mr. Lights Out" Brad Lidge, and like Game 2 of this series, the Sox took advantage. A pinch-hit, yep, that's right, a pinch-hit single by Willie Harris. Like Geoff Blum before him, Harris had one hit in the World Series, and it was, let's say, monstrous. A lead-off single in the eighth against one of the best relief pitchers in the league. Like Podsednik's walk-off a few days earlier, the Sox got to Lidge. Nothing in sports or life is a sure thing. The clichés are correct. It's why you play the game.

These 'second-tier' players shaped the Sox season like few others before or after them. Their stories of how they came to be on the team fascinate as much as their playoff performances. Podsednik was part of a December 2004 hot stove league trade for Carlos Lee, a fan favorite. Harris was a trade acquisition for highly regarded Chris Singleton a few years earlier. They gained Blum for a minor leaguer a few months before his magical moment. All three made their impact felt during the magical season of 2005. But, one of the few free agency signings of 2005 would overshadow all their contributions.

Jermaine Dye agreed to become a White Sox player via free agency. His best years had been behind him after he broke his leg fouling a ball off his knee in an American League Division playoff game in 2001. In the '05 season, Dye performed admirably with 31 home runs and a .274 regular season average. In the Astros' series, he hit over .400 and knocked in 15% of the Sox runs. He was a quiet leader who made a lot of noise in big moments.

He stepped to the plate with two outs in the eight after a sacrifice bunt by, yes, Podsednik, put Harris on third with two outs. Dye laced a single up the middle, and Harris raced home for the 1-0 lead. We were sensing it. Yet, history was looking over our shoulders and snickering. Have all the curses of past summers been dispelled?

The last six outs were frightening. The Astros put together some small ball of their own in the eight. Willy Taveras reached first after being beaned by Cliff Politte and then moved to second on a wild pitch. Enter another unsung reliever in Neal Cotts to snuff the threat. The Sox went quietly in the ninth and summoned the Big Guy for a record-breaking performance. Bobby Jenks was called upon to become the first rookie to close a World Series contest. No other first-year player had ever been on the mound for the clinching final out. Get ready, Cooperstown. But first, there was the catch.

Minute Maid Field's cockamamie design would play a role. There is a trapezoid shape to the stands surrounding the infield. From the third base dugout, the wall juts out diagonally towards the seats, creating a vast, foul territory. Past the infield grass, the fence cuts sharply back at a ninety-degree angle towards the field of play. Any infielders looking to catch a foul ball must be wary. This was the second time the Sox had ever played on this field. None of this mattered to Juan Uribe.

In the stress-filled ninth, the Astros put the tying run on second with one out. There was a pop-up headed toward the stands near third base. Uribe and third baseman Joe Crede chased it as it drifted toward the crowd. Uribe called off Crede and, in full stride, grabbed the ball as his inertia carried him into the stands. "He got it!" Crede seems to mouth. But did he? I couldn't see it.

Players and fans alike were unsure as well. We awaited the umpire's call. The ump needed a closer view and moved right up against the three-foot wall, bent over to look at Uribe's glove, and then told the Astros fans the bad news. With a strong fist pump rising into the Houston air, he ruled he had caught it. Two outs. Don't Stop Believing, but do get in position.

Dan and I made our move. We needed to get behind the Sox dugout in a hurry. We had left our seats at the top of the ninth and headed towards the third baseline. Like in Anaheim, we were getting closer and closer with every pitch and every chair we saw vacated. We couldn't see Uribe's catch as he flew into the stands. We did, however, see his next web gem.

What gets lost in the post-game celebrations is that Juan Uribe made two of the most dazzling late-inning plays back-to-back in baseball history. His leap into the stands to snag the foul ball for out number two was one of the finest defensive plays in White Sox history. His next play was simply magnificent. Orlando Palermo (for you trivia buffs) bounced one just over the head of Bobby Jenks. It slowed and flattened out as it hit the infield grass behind the mound. Uribe charged from short, scooped it, and fired to Paul Konerko at first. It was a bang/bang pick up and throw, and it nailed Palermo by a split second. He was in the air with his last stretch towards the bag when Konerko gloved it. It was close, but he was out. The Sox had ended an 88-year drought, and Konerko pocketed the ball.

An MLB photographer captured the delirium that overtook my brother and me. We have had it reproduced, and it hangs in Dan's basement. In the classic keepsake, we have identical facial expressions. Our right hands are on our respective heads, trying to keep them from exploding. Our jaws are agape. We look tiddly. We had reached sports fans' nirvana. This is what it looked like; what it felt like was even more stirring.

Folks who reach rapture speak of out-of-body experiences. They recall a feeling of keen observation by which they are all seeing. It's the level above happiness where total contentment hangs out. A step up from joy is euphoria. Many avow to achieving this state using mind-altering psychedelics. The idea of gaining such a level of arousal with a community of like-minded souls is beyond one's comprehension. We became united with the White Sox nation, past and present. The Sox were World Champions, and I was there with kindred spirits whom I didn't know by name but knew by the leaning of their hearts.

The players regaled on the field as fans rejoiced in the stands. There was a guy who fashioned himself as Neon Boy, wrapped in a roll of white neon lights you might use for Christmas decorations. I had seen him at a few of the home playoff games. He was still representing the peak of Sox fandom. My hat went off to him for his display of passion. As I acknowledged him, two overly dressed young people emerged from the Sox dugout and headed our way. A street crew from Wheaties came across the aisle. Neon Boy asked me to help him stand up on the seats with us. I grabbed him and helped him stand tall. Just then, the street team handed him and me freshly minted and full boxes of Wheaties with the World Champion White Sox featuring Mark Buehrle on the cover. It was a prized possession that made it back to Chicago but has since vanished.

For now, there was joy in Mudville. My brother and I basked in ecstasy, along with about 200 other pale hose supporters. One by one, the members of the Sox would head to the clubhouse through the dugout and right under the two of us. Each player would make eye contact with us, high five, smile, or provide a tip of a hat to recognize our presence as we recognized their accomplishments. The night belonged to the South Side.

Back home in Chicago, TV stations again broke into regular programming to go live from the field. They again broadcasted my mug back to the homies. My phone shook again as dozens of friends and family saw me. They played out the scene vicariously through us. It was a unifying experience for all. The players came off the field and glanced our way. Looks of mutual respect passed between us, forming a universal bond even though we were complete strangers. Our contentment was being broadcast back to our neighbors, connecting all of us to the moment. I felt the energy of those shared emotions.

Being there had its own invisible touch. It was congealing in our hearts and souls. A bond formed between fans in the stands and the players on the field. They didn't know us, but they knew us at that moment. This was being there. This is what intimacy feels like. Back home in bars or living rooms, the high fives and hugs are fantastic. There is something otherworldly with hugs shared amongst complete strangers. You hug each other tight enough to get to the feeling you both have deep in your soul. Brotherhood, you might call it. When you feel it from a completely unknown human, you connect at a profound level of emotion. It comes up inside you as you greet this like-minded spirit. It sends chills.

The Sox had won this for everyone. Tonight they ride for the diehards who hung on every pitch to the bandwagon jumpers who couldn't name three players. The win was for the police and fire crews, the night watchman, who followed the game on the radio, and the grandparents who lived 87 years and didn't get to feel this day. The cheer echoed through City Hall and flowed to the city's alleys. For devoted fans who never miss an Opening Day to those who select a single game to attend each year on their birthday. The moment belonged to all of them.

Most players had made their way into the locker room for the team celebration. Frozen in delight, the Sox fans in Houston didn't budge. There was a magnetism to the place, keeping us there. Our devotion turned to reward. Mark Buehrle returned to the field with a champagne bottle with one intent. To spray us. Buehrle was a hero if ever there was one. A stud who would later fulfill another bucket list item for me by pitching a perfect game with me in attendance. Good old Number 56 ran up the dugout steps, shook a bottle of champagne, and squirted it in our direction. My eyes never burned so good. An expressive gesture to us worthy fans from a genuine leader. He was christening us into the locker room and connecting the legions of fans back home, traveling esoterically back generations. The champagne soaked through my clothes, into my heart, and into the souls watching back in Flossmoor and the entire Chicago area. This was our championship.

Buehrle's champagne shower washed away decades of almosts and "wait 'til next year" seasons. The bubbly cleansed the representatives of a metropolitan area known as the Second City, but who tonight sat on top of the world. Champions on the field, in the stands, and back home in the Windy. The players had done it, but Buehrle wanted us to know we were also part of it. You don't get that at home. In the arena, you felt the cosmic energy.

Eventually, we got some love from Ozzie Guillén and the others. We saw Jermaine Dye get his MVP car, and then we headed into the streets of Houston, as we did in Anaheim en masse. High fives of shared disbelief and the hugging of my brother remain etched into my memory. I fondly recall the bar where we randomly ran into my cousin Dirty and other friends like the Fordon twins, who shared a birthday with me and now this fabulous moment. It all coalesced that evening—reckless delight. We were no longer visiting fans in Texas. We were children in a playground of joy.

The night seemed to last forever. It had to be because we had no hotel room. After hours of more reveling in Houston's great bars, we drove back to the airport and slept in the car for about two hours before boarding a plane home as the World Champions. We had a parade to see.

The parade was on a school day. I took my kids out of school to attend the once-every-hundred-year civic celebration. They wouldn't be alone in this hooky affair. Your children are in school roughly 200 days a year for 12 years through high school. That's 2,400 days. They can miss one day. My three offspring and three of their friends, Annie Disabato, Elise Smith, and Katie McCormick, hopped on the Metra train into the city. The parade route started at 35th Street, known affectionately as Bill Veeck Drive, and worked its way into the city, passing the south side neighborhoods starting with Bridgeport, home of the Chicago mayoral family, the Daleys. It's also the hood of the White Sox themselves. It seemed like a great place to watch the parade; however, I thought I'd be crashing a private party without an invitation

The neighborhood around Comiskey had a special bond with the team. Residents put up with endless losing seasons and 81 nights a year of streets being blocked with traffic. They endured fans looking for cheap parking while spewing beer cans and urine anywhere they felt. They put up with the relentless banging of plastic pails by desperate buskers every night during long home stands. This Irish-heavy enclave had endured plenty. The two Comiskeys had been in their neighborhood for over a century. They were part of the fabric woven into the stitches on every Sox cap you see. This team is Bridgeport's softball team—think Brooklyn Dodgers kind of attachment. They deserved their own celebration with no interlopers. Though I think the emotion of the Bridgeport section of this parade would have been the highest octane of collective spirit, I did not belong there. It was a neighborhood celebration with lifetime residents holding hands and clenching fists in appreciation of their boys who brought home the flag.

With kids in tow, I headed toward the parade finish. Let the Bridge-porters have their "private ceremony." I was part of the bigger metropolis. We took the Metra train as far as it went and walked down Jackson Boulevard. My 11-year-old son Tommy had his black and white Hulk fist with him. It had become the good luck charm, and it deserved to see the parade.

The civic pride amazed me as we departed the train with dozens of other revelers. The turnout and the happiness were palpable. It was like a movie scene where all the extras play enthralled visitors welcoming aliens from the planet of joy. Bliss was the theme. People were walking hurriedly, making it appear like they were gliding to their locations. The parade would pass our area in an hour's time, and the anticipation was beyond Christmas Eve. It would be like seeing Santa, the Easter Bunny, and the Tooth Fairy

in person lofted high above in red double-decker buses. The real
McCoy's had overcome the Hatfields of major league baseball and
did it before the Cubs. (OK, I had to throw that in, but more on my
genuine emotions later.)

The street was about five deep off the sidewalk as White Sox
nation drew close to see their heroes. The young girls with me
would need a perch. Despite the players being lofted 15 feet above
street level on open-air buses, there was no way they could see
things from that street-level vantage point. I needed to elevate my
group. We walked a few blocks along the route when I spotted a
large window ledge about five feet off the ground. It was a massive
fifteen-foot wide windowsill sticking a foot and a half out of the
building. A perfect ledge for raised viewing. I quickly garnered a
garbage can and helped the kids shimmy their way up to the shelf.
From this roost, we were essentially standing on the shoulders of
the other parade viewers. My only concern was Chicago's finest
feeling, important and telling us to get down. The only cop who
caught my eye just smiled. The six of us waited for the busloads of
our boys to pass us by.

They arrived with tremendous fanfare accented by applause,
catcalls, screams, and exclamations. Hundreds of fans in our
immediate vicinity shrieked with emotion. A glorious release of
scores of years of angst released in a collective mode of euphoria.
It felt very similar to the moment Buehrle soaked us with champagne. Being there in the midst was essential. The noise was a din
of cacophony powered by energy rooted in the temple of goodness.

The parade of double-decker passes passed as fans shouted out
players' names, yelling and jumping. Their fingers outstretched,
seeking magical high fives, connecting with their team. As we
stood balancing on the ledge above the crowd, we spotted the
bus with A.J. Pierzynski and his family. Pierzynski was scanning
the crowd when he locked eyes with my son Tommy. Upon spot-
ting the black Hulk fist, A.J. threw his head back and laughed. He
pointed to Tommy and gave him his version of the fist pump back

to him. Tommy returned the gesture, echoing A.J.'s fist pump with his own. Then A.J. turned to the others on the bus and pointed back our way so they would see this foam fist painted black and white with the Sox-styled logo. Several other players and family members all noticed the fist and pumped their hands in recognition. All laughed and shared the joy across the thirty yards that separated us. We had stood out. The Sox spotted us. My son Tommy was stuck in a state of glee. We had been a part of it. We connected.

The buses passed us, traveling north on LaSalle towards the river. The multitudes had collapsed into the street for the stage ceremony. We caught enough of the pomp to see Konerko take a ball, the last out I watched him catch in Houston, and presented it to the team owner Jerry Reinsdorf. We couldn't hear much from the stage, but we understood the gesture. Witnessing that moment and the recognition from A.J. was enough to fill our days. We floated away from the rest of the pomp and looked for a place to eat. Jubilation filled the streets; the city was in love with itself. No one had a bad word or a care. The energy carried us from one block to the next in search of something to eat. We eventually ended up at Bennigan's on Michigan Avenue. The kids ordered some appetizers and wallowed in the excitement that had just transpired. The day was an accumulation of years. To these very young fans, it meant a great deal; to us older guys, it meant everything.

How could a civic celebration speak to many diverse individuals and make them feel like one? The people that attended that parade and festival were of every race, age, and creed (I assume, though undoubtedly, many of them focused on the religion of baseball). They were young and old. They were Caucasians and African Americans, Asians, and Mexicans. And yet today, they wore the city's colors: black and white.

The city's collective pride manifested itself in individual happiness that metastasized into this glorious communal energy. Spirits elevated. Wishes had come true. A sense of a new pride enveloped the citizens. Chicago's segmented roots came together on this day. The diverse neighborhoods and ethnic enclaves celebrated collectively. There was a familiarity and a recognition of the trials we all endured to get to this moment.

Season after season, we would face our reality as Chicago baseball fans by watching another city's squad loft the silly trophy with all those golden flags. But this year was different. This year was not the same. This was OUR YEAR; we shared it as a city, as a town in a giant block party of raging exhilaration. The world had come to our doorstep to anoint us champions, and we wore it well.

Gone were the regrets of seasons past. We were champions. We had cheered enough. We watched enough West Coast games long past midnight over the years. We drank enough beers as a sixteen-year-old in the old Comiskey and got wet enough with Harry Carey in the centerfield shower. We had stood tall enough when Dick Allen became our starting first baseman. We endured enough parking woes as the new Comiskey conflicted with the destruction of the old Comiskey across the street. We had yelled enough at the television at poor coaching decisions. We strategized enough in the south suburb bars on how to improve the team. We yelled enough to be heard. Our tantrums worked to the end we wanted. We demanded that enough managers get fired, enough free agents get signed, and enough hot dogs get served without ketchup. We had brought our team to this moment, and we reveled in it. The celebration, nearly a century in the making, was complete. We made our way home on the overcrowded train with smiles as long as a Scott Podsednik home run. That is to say, long enough.

Chapter 2

Now All Look Out, Here Come the Hawks

PERIOD 1

My Chicago championship odyssey started with the luck of the draw. I was the fourth child by birth order, and my number was up. My dad was taking me to a Game 7 Stanley Cup Final in the Madhouse on Madison. I was 10 years old and nearly shit in my pants.

My dad owned two season tickets to the Blackhawks and doled them out via his own system. He rotated amongst my siblings in age order without fail. It gave my dad one-on-one time with us on our individual game nights. On May 18, 1971, I was next in line. It was going to be an epic night, and I had lucked into being my dad's seat mate for a winner take all game against the Montreal Canadiens.

In this pre-litigation era of professional sports, it had become a hockey fan tradition to climb onto the ice and celebrate with the team when they win the Cup. This fabled tradition is now only carried out by college students after a shocking home basketball or football win. But back in the day, as they say, it was common for a team to be joined by their fans as they carried the Cup around the home rink. As we drove down, I asked my dad if I would be ok to climb onto the ice after a Hawks' clinching victory. I explained how I would do it. He seemed impressed that I had thought it through. He reserved his answer by saying wisely, "Let's win the game first."

It was a perfect answer. He didn't have to disappoint me with a hard and fast no, yet he left the door open for me. He also gave his snot-nosed son a lesson in counting your chickens before they hatch. The opportunity to jump on the ice and share the Cup with Stan Mikita, Bobby Hull, Dennis Hull, Tony O, and my other heroes seemed like a thrill beyond imagination. That thrill would have to live in my imagination forever.

My dad's season tickets were in the mezzanine on the blue line, where the Hawks shot twice. It was the first time I heard the word mezzanine. (You don't hear that word much, do you?) The old Chicago Stadium was raucous. It was an original playground for old-school hockey. These were the formative years of the madness. Music groups hated performing in the old building because it was acoustically tweaked to amp up the crowd noise during games. Bands performing in the cavernous confines found their sound distorted by the audience's verbal outcries. They found it difficult to hear themselves, not to mention the lack of quality sound for the fans on the main floor where the ice rink usually was. But for watching an original six hockey game, there was no place like it on Earth.

The Hawks jumped to a 2-0 lead in the second period. I think it was midway through the period though that was hard to tell. The Chicago Stadium had one of the trickiest scoreboard clocks of all time. It did not have lighted numbers ticking downward from 20:00 to 0:00 like you see today. The stadium clock ran as a clock. If a clock had 20 hours. It didn't run down; it ran up. Unlike every other scoreboard known to man, the stadium clock did not reveal the time left in the period, but it ran as a reflection of how much time had expired.

I'll try to explain this craziness. There were two hands on the poorly lit scoreboard. The larger of the two stood at zero or what we would consider the twelve on an analog clock. The second hand rotated rapidly around the face. It took 60 seconds to complete the circumference. The hour hand, which was really the minute hand, would slide slowly toward the next number; however, it went from 20 to zero.

Figuring the clock out was a mental challenge. If you looked up at it and it looked like it was 3:30 in the afternoon, it meant that five and a half minutes had expired, and there were 14 and a half minutes left in the period. You had to deduce that in the middle of a game to figure out how much time remained in a period. The quarter stops of the clock were not three, six, nine, or 12 as on a standard clock but 5, 10, 15, and 20. There was no hour hand, only a minute and seconds hand that told time as it was being played, not how much time remained. It was tough sledding for a 10-year-old to keep track. Not to mention the confusion of the much smaller circles that function in the same way for penalties. You thought the manual scoreboard at Wrigley Field was primitive? Eventually, you'd grasp it; however, I'd imagine the players had quite a fit trying to figure it out in the heat of a game.

One thing for sure was it was in the second period of Game 7 that the Hawks took a two-goal lead. Then comes a moment that epitomizes momentum change. The dump-in turned into the shot that changed the complexion of a champion. The Canadiens' Jacques Lemaire, a very average player, sent in a very average slap shot from center ice. A shot usually deflected easily by the goalie and sent to their defense while the players changed lines. This time, it went in. The Madhouse went silent. A noiseless gasp cleared the stadium of joy in a breath. The lead was still one-goal, but something had changed. The world had a hiccup on its axis. Atlas shrugged.

The Canadiens quickly scored again as the much despised but greatly respected Henri 'Rocket' Richard tied the game before the second stanza ended. A stunned crowd didn't move during the intermission. We didn't know what had happened. A 2-0 lead in a Stanley Cup Final should be untouchable in the defensive-strong 1970s brand of hockey. The tight-checking playing style that prevailed in the finals usually meant a two-goal lead in your home building was insurmountable. Despite the tied score, Hawks fans felt like we were losing. I sensed the players felt the same.

The third period started with more ridiculous antics by the two goalies before the Canadiens snuck another one past Espo. The air in the stadium left through the large vents in the ceiling that no one ever knew what they were there for, anyway. Tonight, there would be no jumping on the ice as the visitors would hoist the oldest trophy in sport. I would not get the chance to scale the plexiglass separating the players from the crowd. There was no madness, only sadness, in the Madhouse on Madison. The Canadiens were champions, and the Blackhawks were bridesmaids. A scar remained on my still-developing cerebrum. A night of promise had dissolved into despair.

To this 10-year-old, it was a moment that forced him to chase his dream for over five decades. The emptiness drove me to New Orleans to watch the Bears in Super Bowl XX on a whim. It empowered me to drop everything and blow off a friend's complimentary tickets to an NFL skybox in favor of a trip to Anaheim to watch a pennant-clinching baseball game. It also drove me 38 years later to grab my son and board a plane to Philadelphia despite the threat of violence to overcome the disappointment of this evening. The sorrow had dug a hole that took years to fill.

The Hawks blew a two-goal lead. Afterward, we didn't blame Bartman nor the goalie Esposito for letting one sneak by him from center ice. It was a collapse that left us wanting more. We thought the Hawks were like the Canadiens dynasty before them, built for the long haul. They would make two finals appearances in three years. After that, they would not return to the championship for two decades. This night, as gloomy as we were, we left the game thinking they drove one of the best teams in the history of hockey to seven games before succumbing. They had a roster of young-sters who would be hungry for, you guessed it, "next year."

That hunger wasn't enough. Despite one of the best team songs ever written (kudos to Percy Faith and his Orchestra), the Hawks began a nerve-racking series of playoff runs that came up tantalizingly short. This stacked team of hockey legends failed to deliver their fans to the promised land. This run of almosts became known as the Arthur Wirtz era. After a promising start, it went on way too long.

Arthur Wirtz had been a silent partner and became the team's sole owner following James D. Norris's death in 1966. Wirtz inherited a team that had won the Stanley Cup five years earlier. (A Cup won in Detroit over the rival Red Wings when I was two days old.) Wirtz started things off with one of the worst trades in Chicago sport's history. In what is ironically referred to as 'Wirtz Wisdom,' the Hawks sent Phil Esposito, Ken Hodge, and Fred Stanfield to Boston for what we like to say was a bag of pucks. In exchange, the Hawks received one decent player: Pit Martin. The other two players, Jack Norris (no relation) and Gilles Marotte lasted less than three years with the Hawks. They were no longer on the Hawks when Esposito and Hodges led the Bruins to one of the most storied runs in hockey history as they skated into the Hall of Fame.

Wirtz somehow stumbled into a run of success in the 1970s. After an expansion of the league moved the Hawks to the weaker West Division, a series of long playoff runs ensued. The Hawks took advantage of an easier route to the finals and thus made them two out of three years representing the Western Conference. Then they slid back to mediocrity. They made the playoffs every year of the decade and every year but twice went home without making the Finals. In those last two appearances, they ran into the same team: Montreal. And in those same two series, they ran into the same brick wall: Ken Dryden.

When the Hawks entered the 1971 playoffs, Ken Dryden had played only six regular season games in the NHL. His six-foot-plus stature made him more of a freak show than a potential Hall of Famer. He changed the game. Before his rise to prominence, goalies were mostly smaller players who usually lacked the physicality to play as forwards. They also had names like Gump or Cesare. They were famous, of course, to hockey fans; however, no one would ever consider them physical athletes of stature. Ken Dryden changed all that.

The rookie Dryden was also a college graduate—seemingly unheard of for a hockey player, let alone a goalie. The Cornell graduate had come out of nowhere in the first round of the playoffs by shutting down the fabled Boston Bruins—one of the NHL's all-time great offensive juggernauts. Phil Esposito led the Bruins with 76 goals and an under appreciated 76 assists. The defense of Bobby Orr—he of 100 plus points fame—made the Boston squad the Stanley Cup favorites in 1971. Two other Bruins, Hodges and Johnny Bucyk, also tallied over 100 points. The Bruins might lose a game; however, they were going to score. That is, unless the rookie starting just his seventh game in the bigs was Ken Dryden. Dryden stopped the Bruins cold and helped the Canadiens advance to the finals by beating an overmatched Minnesota North Stars team.

Dryden's first Cup, the one I witnessed in person, drew a few million people on TV. The game had such an impact that CBS preempted regular programming to provide the game a nationwide audience—something that was unique at the time. That victory was the last of 10 for Canadiens' legend Jean Béliveau and the first of six for Dryden. His trendsetting size and success made general managers fleece the country for tall, mobile goalies. The strategy echoed in other sports as taller athletes became de rigueur.

Dryden was a physical specimen that changed how they designed hockey teams and had a lasting impression on all sports. Soon after Dryden's arrival and sterling success, all major sports began emphasizing physical size and strength when building their teams. The NHL of the early 1970s comprised crafty, short, stocky men willing to lose some teeth to score a goal. They were not the future of hockey or any other sport. Gump Worsley was a Hall of Fame goalie. He was five-foot-seven inches tall with skates on. Today, he couldn't start on a standard Minnesota high school team because of his size. The physicality of sport was changing, and Ken Dryden was on the cutting edge of that sea change. It was just too bad he played for the Canadiens. Dryden set other standards for athletes' post-career ambitions, too. All six-foot-four of him went on to a myriad of successes after his playing days ended. The underappreciated legend is now the Officer of the Order of Canada and a former cabinet minister, amongst other accomplishments, including writing one of the finest sports memoirs of all time.

Now there wasn't much shame in losing to the Canadiens. It was like dropping a playoff game to a Tom Brady–led team. The Canadiens were a recurring dynasty composed of a series of dominant players of the era. This Canadiens dynasty won seven of ten Cups played between 1969 and 1979.

It would be easy for Blackhawks fans to blame a curse like the Cubs' black cat of 1969 or to rally on social media as they would today to call for the head of the future Hall of Fame goalie who had a momentary lapse of greatness. No one turned this into a plague of historic proportions or rallied the ruffians to charge the gate and burn down Versailles. We simply sat stunned for nearly a lifetime.

My dad continued to be a season ticket owner as the Hawks went on a pretty impressive roll of playoff appearances throughout the 1970s and into the early 1980s. They managed one more Finals appearance two years later with similar results. The 1973 Finals featured a couple of mad shootouts. One game saw a record-setting eight goals in a period. Unfortunately, the Hawks lost another Stanley Cup Final to the Canadiens. I watched it at home with Peter Puck.

PERIOD 2

The Blackhawks of the 1970s were competitive and exciting. They filled the stadium each night with suit-wearing gentlemen and a few women entertained by the tempo of a live hockey game. In the cement hallways of the mezzanine section, the scent of cigars permeated the well-dressed fans. Never late to their seats for the start of a period, they were experiencing the evolution of the sport from a tightly played defensive struggle to a wide-open affair that crescendoed with Wayne Gretzky's high-flying Edmonton Oilers of the 1980s.

Along with bell bottoms and disco, the Blackhawks and the Boston Bruins of the 1970s ushered in a new era of hockey. Shooters and scorers created a more up-tempo style of play. Bobby Hull made his mark during this era with a wicked slap shot and the league's earliest curved stick. Growing up watching these players, we not only wished to emulate their scoring ways, but we also wanted to look like them. When The Golden Jet Hull heated his stick blade to put a slight curve in the wood for better puck handling, we did the same. This tiny geometric change to his equipment would allow for significantly more velocity and accuracy in his shots. Science had invaded the game and all of sport.

Hull's innovation led to a plethora of goals and, eventually, rule changes concerning stick curvature. It was, in fact, a compromise. League officials struggled with Hull's innovation (an idea borrowed from teammate Stan Mikita). His colossal goal totals were having a positive impact on the game with fans. As sticks resembled boomerangs, goalie health was becoming a growing concern with the potential of 20-goal games. A curved stick brought such advancement to the game that it had to be reined in. Yet, abolishing it entirely would mean clamping down on an element of the game that had brought excitement to the fans. As the goaltenders like Dryden, became better and better, the need to arm the shooters with better instruments also became necessary. The compromise was to allow curves up to a limit.

At home, we needed to learn how to bend our sticks for ourselves, as stick manufacturers had not caught up to the trend yet. We'd heat our sticks in the garage using dangerous Bunsen burners, attempting to create our own "banana blades." This epic change in sticks to young aspiring hockey players was like introducing metal woods to golf amateurs. You just became better overnight.

Curving your hockey stick was a way to add speed and control to your stick handling and shooting skills. It raised your game based on simple technology. If you ever doubt this, try using a straight-blade hockey stick (if you can find one). Trying to control the puck with a straight blade is like driving an old-fashioned persimmon wood off the fairway. You may get lucky once.

Overnight, the game had changed, and we at home spent hours mimicking it. We did more than curve our sticks to be like Bobby. My brother John and I changed the way we shot. With flat sticks, it mattered little which wing you played—on the right or left. It was a matter of which hand was at the top of the stick near the crazily taped butt of the stick. If your right hand was on the top of the stick, you were a left-hand shot. My brother was a right-hand shot until Hull changed the game. He immediately changed to become a lefty. When I left goaltending to become a forward, I, too, converted to a lefty. Simply because Bobby Hull was a lefty.[1]

Hull's history with the Black Hawks didn't end well. He again became a symbol of things to come. Shortly after the Hawks lost that epic seventh game in front of the home crowd, Hull took his 118-mph snapshot to the World Hockey Association (WHA).

---

1   As a caveat to this stick diversion, we once secured an actual game-used stick of Bobby Hull's before the rule changes. He curved his blade to such a degree that if you laid it on the ground, you could sneak a tennis ball under it. There must have been a three-inch bend. Imagine the speed one could generate on a puck with that much curve.

Hull's departure was a front-page story that crushed my 11-year-old sports fan's heart. He did the unthinkable. The press called Hull's financial decision treason. Or so the Wirtz family tried to portray it. As the ugly soap opera played out, it traumatized this young fan. Why would anyone leave my team? I would play for the Hawks for free.

The concept of free agency was in its infancy. Baseball's Curt Flood's reserve clause case had been winding its way through the court system. Few experts or fans thought the player would win his freedom to choose what team he played on. To us fans, we faced a dilemma ourselves. Was a player to remain loyal to his team? Or could he practice the freedom available to every other employee in America? The right to choose where you ply your trade?

The Bobby Hull free agency ordeal was lame compared to today's frequent team hopping. In 1972, it was outlandish. Bobby Hull was a top scorer in the NHL, and many say he was one of the most formidable sons of bitches ever to play the game. He frequently fought, and he often scored. Goalies admitted the terror they felt when he was ready to shoot. He was at his peak as a player. Subsequently, he won a couple of MVPs and two championship rings in the fledgling WHA after he split open my heart by splitting from the Blackhawks.

Today's professional athletes owe much to Curt Flood and Bobby Hull[2]. The curious side of Flood's case was he was trying to stay on the Cardinals by refusing a trade. Hull was looking for financial security. He wanted a long-term deal from stingy management (Arthur Wirtz era). The idea of a player refusing any offer in the late 1970s was still pretty absurd and considered ungracious.

---

2   Hull remains an enigma. His off the ice antics during his career and after it remain a sordid tale. Heroes tend to create real moral dilemmas for fans. A topic I'd like to explore more in the future, but will leave it to rest here. Hull's off-ice behavior can not be condoned. I present my emotions as a teenager looking for heroes.

Many fans sided with management and ownership regarding players jumping teams. Free agency became a right despite the emotional havoc it played with fans' allegiances.

The flood of free agency started with a Flood. In his argument that eventually reached the highest court in the land, the St. Louis Cardinal centerfielder argued that the tenured sports professional's career was akin to indentured servitude. Flood was voicing his individualism and claiming his constitutional right to choose. Most shamed Flood for his stance. He would lose his case in the US Supreme Court, giving truth to the expression of losing the battle but eventually winning the war for all professional athletes.

Hull and Flood based their arguments on different criteria, but the key point was the same: a player's right to choose. Hull's departure was part of a grander scheme, as every team in the WHA agreed to pay his salary. In baseball, no one paid Flood's. Hull became a tool of the owners of one league rallying against the owners of another. Both leagues of baseball shunned Flood. He had to spend years in court. Hull just had to fly to Winnipeg, causing me a great deal of heartache. Flood's case was one of the old sentinels' schemes of trying to protect their way of doing business. Hull's was a case study of disrupters changing an industry.

Hull's departure should have sent shock waves through Blackhawks' ownership the way the newspapers should have used their profits as a trailblazer on the Internet. Instead, they chose to make Hull the bad guy. Hull suggested in interviews that his goal was to sign a long-term deal of $250,000 a year with the Hawks. The WHA offered him $1,000,000 for four years. Hull said he took the deal because even if the league cratered in its inaugural season, he would have come out with his quarter of a million. They didn't. Hull made out and received all his money. The WHA became a competitive league before eventually being sucked up into the NHL.

It's interesting to explore the idea of Hull's salary being subsidized by all the teams. Though it might violate some anti-trust laws, it highlights how cooperation can make great things happen. Teams that would fight it out on the ice for supremacy realized the importance of the league as the top priority. The WHA owners were trendsetters. Other leagues that have risen as competition to the established ones have often failed. We can list the successes on one hand—the AFL in football, the ABA in basketball and some might say, the American League in baseball. Most new leagues (think USFL) have failed miserably because they focused on competing internally. Teams that fought each other in the league routinely imploded. The unified front of WHA owners backed Hull's plan and made it work. Today, an arrangement of companies in the same industry joining forces to combat external business forces might find its day in court. The WHA pulled a fast one on the status quo by making business more expensive for NHL owners while changing the game for fans.

The bottom line to us true-blooded Hawks fans was simple; it devastated us. Fresh off their 1971 Finals appearance (one they would repeat without Hull in '73, showing you how good this team was), the Hawks seem primed for a dynasty of their own. The Wirtz family hoarded their cash and ignored the sea change of sports finances. With the benefit of being placed in a weaker conference, the Hawks continued to make the playoffs; however, they only won three playoff series in the next eight years. Instead of heeding the winds of change to continue to compete, the Wirtz family chose mediocrity. It took us fans a long time to realize what was happening.

There would be grand moments and miraculous playoff runs powered by Denis Savard and Jeremy Roenick. Still, there would be just one more Finals appearance during the lean years of 1974-2000. In the 1992 playoffs, the Hawks met a supercharged Pittsburgh Penguins team at the beginning of their apex. Behind Mario Lemieux, the Penguins swept the Hawks before Chicago's bandwagon could get backed up to add casual fans. It was a pleasant run, and with it, a peek at the Cup, though that didn't last either. The Blackhawks of the 1990s were flat-out miserable, winning only three playoff rounds and missing the playoffs nine times over the next 15 years. Arthur Wirtz died in 1983. His son, William, continued their infuriating strategies. The ongoing era had exhausted us all.

It was the end of this Hawk fan's dedication and financial contributions. After multiple years of missing the playoffs and watching season ticket prices go up (they professed to have a waiting list for season tickets still), I wanted out. The non-renewal of my tickets ended a multi-decade run as a supporter who attended dozens of games a year. I pretended my decision was my miniature statement to ownership to improve the product. It was more complicated than that.

My decision was timing and finances. My brother continued to purchase tickets as a business tool. Meanwhile, my business saw little value in the 'investment.' Raising kids and running a business, I found it ever so challenging to make it out on a school night for a meaningless game in the middle of January. I was ok with losing out on playoff options. It was a non-factor since they missed the playoffs every year but one from 1998 to 2008. Season tickets are incredibly costly, and you still needed to pay in advance for any potential playoff march. Suppose you didn't pay for those four rounds of playoffs despite the team only advancing beyond three rounds once in three decades; well, sorry, Charlie. In that case, they might sell your season tickets out from under you.

It's quite a quandary for a fan. It leaves a lot of ardent fans cheering from home. Sports owners profit immensely from their season ticket base. Owners can park their money in interest pools by securing revenue in advance from their most vital fans. Fans are forced to decide if committing sizable sums of cash for a season you are lucky to make only 40% of the games is worth it. And for what? Mediocrity? What fans should demand is forward progress on the field.

I cannot argue with individuals and corporations that pay for season tickets. They forego oodles of cash for entertainment;

however, when management cannot perform or appears to be going cheap, they should be called out. Fans should organize boycotts of games or concessions. Good luck, though. Sports teams have their fans right where they want them, and they take full advantage.

I listened to the 1992 Stanley Cup Finals on the radio while playing 16-inch softball—another fine Chicago sports tradition. The Hawks became the first team in 48 years to blow a three-goal lead in game one. The Penguins manhandled the Hawks in game two. They came home with little momentum and less energy. Game 3 was a shutout won by the visitors. Game 4 had the thrill of Blackhawks Dirk Graham's hat trick, but that excitement would be short-lived as the Penguins outscored the Hawks 6-5 to win back-to-back Cups. We played a softball game, had the radio on, and sensed the outcome before it happened. The better team won.

The Hawks would not win another playoff series for three years. They would win only five series over the next 16 years. This included a string of missing the playoffs nine out of ten years, which in hockey is like playing golf without going into a sand trap—it's tough to achieve. It was a mess of belt-tightening, wasted talent, coaching changes, and overall lousy management. Then, the old man died.

The two elder Wirtzes appear to have been good businessmen. Though they also seem to be jerks. I, of course, never met them and, in full disclosure, drew all my biased opinions of them from the press reports and my discerning eye on the results. The Wirtz legacy, from the outside, looks like cheap guys that got lucky a few years but mostly thrived on the season ticket base and refused to modernize. Their teams of the late 1960s and early 1970s were as strong as any team in the league. They were consistent contenders and hoisted the Cup once (1961). Those teams had Stan Mikita,and two Hall of Fame goalies. When the time to pay these players to stick around, the Wirtz clan clammed up. Their response relegated the Hawks to second-division status.

The series of general managers who were confidants of Wirtz were 'yes' men to a tee. The very definition of a 'yes' man was Bob Pulford. Pulford was a motionless artifact of another generation. He could not relate. After the Penguins beat down the Hawks, he missed the boat on the new and improved style of play the Penguins were progenitors of, – speed, size, and puck-handling skills. Instead, we loaded up on defense. We failed to compete.

Bill Wirtz also failed the fans. He was notorious for his anti-television rants. The Blackhawks refused to air home games on local TV. Let me repeat this line. For decades, they did not televise the Chicago Blackhawks' home games in *Chicago*. It was an absurdity that became sublime.

Wirtz justified his preposterousness by claiming his season ticket base needed protection. They paid to go to the games, so they should be the only ones to witness them. He didn't realize that he perpetuated a snobbery element in his season ticket holders as well as alienated the potential hundreds of thousands of Chicagoans who wanted to watch the team play in their home Reds. Wirtz calculated that his passionate fans would reward him with what? They were already paying for their seats. It might have been a novel idea to protect your ardent and most affluent supporters, but to what end?

Did he really think season ticket holders would abandon the team if the Blackhawks joined all other professional clubs and began broadcasting their games from home ice? Au contraire. Their tickets would increase in value since more fans would desire to see a live match in the cherished stadium because of the excitement those fans brought to every game. It's unconscionable to think that this went on for years. This wasn't an older man calculating wrong and righting the ship a couple of years later. For nearly two decades, you could not watch a Blackhawks home game on TV.

My family and I have been season ticket holders for many years. We found the ban on TV repulsive. Not once did I feel like I was being cheated by the game being broadcast back home. Many times, for whatever reason, I'd have to miss a home game. As if that's not bad enough, I couldn't even catch it on TV? That was far more frustrating and insulting to us season ticket purchasers. The whole policy just left a foul taste in our mouths. This isn't to say that if they broadcasted home games, there would have been more Stanley Cups. Not at all. However, when ownership is so stuck on asinine policies like not letting your most loyal fan base see a game, who knows what cockamamie decisions they were making behind closed doors that genuinely impacted the outcomes of the matches?

But this story of my Chicago sports Mt. Rushmore of witnessing championships may never have happened if the old geezer didn't pass. In his place came the prodigal son; an offspring who waited patiently in the wings and then, as if on cue, altered everything. Thus, the Rocky Wirtz era began.

As I write this, the once spotless resume of Rocky's tenure has taken on severe rust. His run as boss of the Hawks is, of course, a sordid tale. The Rocky era has turned into a slog of misconduct and pretentious privilege that harmed young men. Recent history has not been too kind to Rocky and his ignorant support staff that perpetrated an inexcusable cover-up. Though his integrity has taken a hit of late, for one brief shining moment, Rocky could do no wrong. Hawk Nation's aspirations rose. That this fall from grace happened to a man that had made lemonade from the lemons his father left him makes it even more bittersweet.

Individuals are complex in sports, politics, or the national spotlight, and our reaction to their behavior is all in one direction - Guilty or not guilty. Yet, it's much more nuanced. If an athlete starts his or her career as a good person with the best intentions and positive on-field results and then falters under different societal morals, should we shun them forever for their misgivings? Do we ignore their transgressions and focus on their good side? Is forgiveness something we need to practice with individuals we neither know personally nor professionally, but just through news reports or TV shows?

As I write this, Wirtz is being criticized in the press for a recent outburst during a town hall meeting with Blackhawk leadership and fans. Wirtz refused to answer questions concerning a recent revelation that management was aware of a male-on-male rapist in the team's coaching ranks. A video coach, with influence, took advantage of a young potential player's aspirations and raped him in his condo, according to documented accusations by the victim. The young prospect made the allegations to the Blackhawks' management as they prepared for their first of three playoff runs in the 2010s. Hawks administration tabled any action on the allegations until the playoffs were over—a playoff run that resulted in the first Stanley Cup Finals victory in 50 years. The team chose to sit on the information in a meeting attended by the club's president, several coaches, and the personal director. (This is according to an internal audit report from a firm hired by the team.)

It was bad enough that they didn't act right away. What made things worse was the team, knowing full well that said accused video coach was under severe allegations of a crime, did nothing after the playoff run ended in Philadelphia. In fact, they exacerbated the situation by making the accused a big part of the team's subsequent celebrations. They permitted him to take part in all post-championship parties, including appearing on stage at the city-wide parade, and bestowed upon him the most special day in any player's dreams: a day with the Cup. The fabled tradition allows each team member, staff, and coach to spend roughly 24 hours with the Cup.

It all amounted to deplorable decision-making by the Blackhawks' management. How could they allow the alleged rapist to have his day with the Cup despite the allegations against him? The team eventually dismissed him (not without a positive recommendation letter from Blackhawks management, which remains suspect and anonymous). None of this surfaced until years later when the victim sued. Then, everything came rushing out 10 years after the fact, just like Watergate—the cover-up that doomed many.

The team might have been able to hide the affair for the week of the Stanley Cup Finals and then reacted, and they may have been fine. Their reckless disregard for the victim's charges went on for weeks well into the end of the summer of 2010. It showed cowardice on behalf of the Blackhawks' front office. They could have avoided all of this. Now the team will pay cash settlements, and some men will pay with their livelihoods. Even Rocky Wirtz's record has been tainted because he couldn't control his emotions after being asked a much-anticipated question. The question he blew up on was tame by most accounts: "What are you doing to prevent such an occurrence in the future?"

Wirtz's press blow-up shattered the team's momentum toward restoring the public's trust. Wirtz's deference wiped away the positive emotions and energy surrounding his name and tenure overseeing the Blackhawks. As his son prepares to take the helm of one of the oldest family sports businesses in the country, he does so with significant baggage. Meet the new boss same as the old boss? Business is tricky, and human emotions are complex. It isn't easy making the right decision. Doing the right thing at the right time can be painful. However, concealing the hurt causes the pain to linger and grow. The healing takes all that much longer. Think Penn State University football.

Dozens of players and coaches knew nothing of the allegations. They focused on the game of hockey and their drive to end five decades of misery for the Blackhawks faithful. I was one of those professed followers, and I enjoyed the ride. Still, my experience feels diminished by these recent developments. Why can't institutions or organizations right the ship by doing the right thing when needed?

No one would diminish the Hawks' accomplishments if they had handled the allegations quietly at, or near the time, the charges presented themselves. Putting the accused on leave of absence while investigating may have solved a great deal. Protecting him and not the victim was a horrendous mistake that took the shine off the accomplishments of an amazing group of hockey players who were a powerful force for a decade. So, though I write my recollections in the cloud of despairing truths, it was a hell of a ride to watch this team achieve the ultimate.

PERIOD 3

In the spring of 2010, my father went to the hospital for the last time. He had turned 81 in February of that year and his health had become one incident after another. By this stage, he had already lived to be older than both of his parents and two of his brothers. He had put significant focus on his personal wellbeing for years. Up to this point, he had prevailed through many diseases and ailments. He had fought though a heart attack, cancer, Parkinson's and crippling depression. However, this time, he had enough. In early May, when the doctors presented him with an optional surgery to correct one more wrong, he said. "I want to go home."

That house was the new home he custom built for him and my mom. Months earlier, they made the move from the home they raised their seven kids in, to a house they built for their new phase of life as grandparents. My dad, who lived in nine different homes before he turned twenty, essentially raised us in one house where he lived for forty years on Sunset Avenue in Flossmoor. Now he returned from the hospital to a new home he declared to be perfect.

My entire family gathered for a weekend vigil as my dad rested in his hospice bed. Thirty of his offspring ate, laughed, prayed and cried together for nearly seventy hours. We watched Dustin Byfuglien, a junior teammate of my nephew John, score a game winning goal as the Blackhawks defeated the San Jose Sharks in Game 1 of the Western Conference Finals.

Throughout the weekend, my dad would have moments of clarity as each of us took turns spending final moments with him. He began asking for his sister, Dolly, who was already on a flight from California. When my dad was six years old and sent to first grade he refused to go. His parents tried everything to provoke him to attend. When he did go, he cried the entire time. At a lost for a solution, they determined that his older sister Veronica, known as Dolly, should retake first grade so she could be with her little brother. They went through the next nine years of schooling as twins. My dad never forgot the gesture. When Dolly arrived at the vigil for my dad. She wept and entered his room. They had some private moments and then he passed.

On the day he died, the Hawks beat the Sharks again and five days later advanced to their first Stanley Cup Final since 1992. They would face the Philadelphia Flyers in a best of seven. The first five games went to the home teams. The Blackhawks held a three games to two lead. Game 6 of the 2010 Stanley Cup Final was to be held in Philadelphia. I attended a few home games during their terrific playoff run, mostly courtesy of my brothers and their tickets. My thought was to withhold my cash savings until I was sure the Cup was in their grasp. This moment came when they defeated the Flyers at home in Game 5, setting the table for history on the ice.

I did what I had done circa 2005 for the White Sox run. I called my brother. This moment must have meant more to John than anyone. Years earlier, he happily paid for the hotel and air-fares to Minneapolis to watch the Dino Ciccarelli–led and hated North Stars defeat our Hawks in the conference playoffs. As a doting father, he bought equipment and paid team fees for his three hockey-crazy sons, who played through their college years. He was invested. His passion for the game and this team had cost him thousands of dollars in season tickets over two decades. In the words of Denis Savard, he committed to the Indian.

It would mean the world to him, and there was no one I wanted to share the moment with more than him. I took the lead by purchasing tickets to the game online in advance. I looked into airfares and called John with the package signed, sealed, and delivered. Unlike the White Sox seat-of-the-pants playoff experiences, airlines, hotels, and tickets were prearranged for the Hawks. I was leaving nothing to chance on this day. All he had to do was come along.

He didn't want to come.

Philadelphia sports fans are reputed to be brutal to the opposing team's supporters. You cheer for the visitors at your own risk in Philly. There had been tales of Mets fans being beaten up at Phillies games. Stories abound about opposing team enthusiasts being pelted with debris at games and then practically beaten to death outside the stadiums after games, so the fanciful fable ran; as if the Broad Street Bullies were a real street gang and showing up in the opposition's colors on their turf was cause for death.

I had visions of the scene from the fantastic movie *Warriors*. Being falsely accused of instigating a riot, the Warriors get threatened at every turn on their journey home from a gang summit. Leaving the stadium after a Philadelphia game sounded like a fight of survival to get to your car. The wearing of Blackhawks' colors marked us as targets, and nowhere would be safe. Run for your lives! It's hard to overemphasize how Philadelphia fans became stereotyped as ogres handing out punishment to all enemy fans. It was a complete bunk.

Though they were not, they had reason to be as nasty as the soccer hooligans from across the ocean. The Flyers' supporters have endured heartbreak unlike any fan base short of the Buffalo Bills. Their hockey team had been to five previous Stanley Cup Finals and lost them all, topping the Chicago born Hall of Fame hero Marv Levy and his Buffalo Bills of the early 1990s. Since winning back-to-back Cups in 1973-74 seasons, the Flyers were facing elimination in the Finals for the sixth time in a row. That had to be frustrating. The thought that their fans may get upset and take it out on an opposing team's fandom was reasonable but far-fetched.

With that urban legend hanging in the air, John turned down my invitation. He could not make it and hung on to the hope of a Blackhawks' loss forcing an ultimate Game 7 back in Chicago, which he had tickets for. My heart sank. I had an extra ticket—time for history to repeat. Decades earlier, I had lucked into a seat with my dad for the 1971 Finals. Now, my son would get the nod for a potential Cup-clinching night.

The magnitude of the event resonated. Even though the cost of the trip doubled, the experience would triple. Being with my son for that clinching game would be something to cherish. Gone was the option of running on the ice with the team but seeing a Hawks team finish the season with a Cup, with my son, had emotional weight. Circle of life. It's something sports can bring. The generational pull echoes through the decades of cheering and jeering. The shouts from the rafters ring through my half-century of being a fan. On this night, I would hear them as the conduit from my dad to my son.

The game was as intense as any Cup Finals game. The action was vigorous. Momentum swung back and forth. My son Tommy and I were edge-of-seat the entire game and quite comfortable despite being surrounded by Flyers fans everywhere. Unlike Anaheim and Houston for the baseball series, seeing a fellow Chicago fan in Philly was a rare sighting—at least one confident and brave enough to wear the Indian head garb.

As the game progressed, we made friends with our fellow hockey buffs in our section. We shared a mutual respect for the team we were playing. As the game entered overtime, my nerves wrecked me. A goal for the Flyers now would crush us and make our multi-hundred-dollar spree a silly jaunt to Philadelphia in the spring. A Blackhawks' goal would cement the memory for a lifetime and cloud out the fifty-plus years of dismal fortune for the beloved Hawks and us faithful followers.

When the moment came, no one recognized it. At a game, I pay intense attention to it. Constantly aware of the situation, I prefer intense watching to chitchatting. Yet, I was confused and uncertain when it all finally happened. I distinctly recall the emotion and confusion of Patrick Kane's rush to the net. At that moment, Kane understood my dad's signature statement of achieving success, "You can't get a hit unless you swing the bat." Kane revealed the inner truth of the cliche: "You can't score unless you shoot the puck."

I can conjure up the sequence in my mind. The Hawks' Brian Campbell keeps the puck in the zone. He sends to Kane along the boards. A quick move finds him deep in the Philadelphia zone. Too deep? He is free at the bottom of the face-off circle. He doesn't shoot the puck as much as he slides it from the weakest of angles. It vanishes.

Is it under the goalie's pads? Is it stuck in a part of his equipment? I always look to the goal judge light in these uncertain moments. Though considered pretty obsolete these days, goal judges used to carry a lot of weight. Their responsibility is to switch the red light on once they see the puck cross the red line (completely crossed, by the way). They would flash the red light, and a celebration would ensue. (Video review has diminished their role). With pent-up energy, I looked to the goal judge light. Darkness. No light and still no puck. The moment itself lasted about three seconds. The suspense created a sensation of time being suspended in a distant reality. Life became frozen over the Forum in Philadelphia. It was 50 years waiting for the blink of an eye.

No one in the rink knew what happened except for one man: Patrick Kane. I looked away from the goal judge and over to Kane. By now, his momentum had taken him around the net and near the opposite face-off circle. The red light did not illuminate; Kane's reaction did. His strip tease became etched on my retina permanently.

I watched him drop his stick, throw off his gloves, and dance as he reached the top of the face-off circle in the Flyers' zone. It was the sign I was waiting for. I grabbed my son in my arms and shouted, "We won the Cup! We won the Cup!" I think he was like thousands of others at that exact moment: "Did we?"

All uncertainty was abated as Kane rushed down the ice to embrace the Hawks' goalie in celebration. The visitors emptied the bench. There was no doubt. After the most prolonged pregnant pause in sports history, all heaven broke loose. Kane knew where the puck was. He had to glimpse it as he skirted behind the net, following his push of the puck. It appeared to everyone that Kane might have been losing his mind. Hawks' captain Jonathan Toews would say later he didn't know it was in, either.

As the celebration moved in slow motion across the ice, the moment became surreal in the stands. They had done it. As the Flyers stood around preparing for the greatest sports tradition (the post-Finals handshake), my son and I were glowing in glee. The Flyers' fans near us reached out to us in congratulations and wished us well. They were most gracious in defeat. We were bonkers in victory.

If the possibility had existed, my son and I would have jumped on the ice that night as I had wished my dad and I could have after Game 7 nearly four decades ago. Notwithstanding, like the White Sox victories on the road, we had better access to the post-game celebrations. As the Flyers fans exited, we made our way around to the Hawks' bench and near ice level as the team took their victory laps with the Cup held high in hand.

The Blackhawks had ended the drought, and my sports magic streak continued. My confidence and risk-taking paid off. A calculated risk to purchase tickets, airfare, and hotel (this time) delivered a lifetime memory of happiness, and ecstatic joy shared with my 16-year-old son, a feeling that I can still conjure up with meditation. I sense the surroundings as I envision that sudden emotion caused by Kane's equipment strip tease. I can conjure up a shot of adrenaline at watching it again on YouTube from a camera angle similar to our perspective. When I hold the paper ticket stub in my hand a decade later, I am exhilarated. We were the champions, and I was there to smell the champagne again.

Though trivial details remain lost, such as the hotel we stayed at, much more persists in fondness. I recall the moment Kane dropped that stick and threw off those gloves with perfect clarity. He was shedding the defeats, the almosts, and the near misses of a lifetime. That night, he stopped the shot Esposito whiffed on in game seven in 1971, and he was bringing Savard, Makita, and Eddie Olczyk across the goal line. He was an individual skater lifting the weight of decades of defeats in an instant. You could feel it inside the Forum (Wachovia Center) that night. Our past was dismissed.

Years before this night, after dealing with another season of disappointment from the Blackhawks, I thought my life would end on the day the Hawks won a Cup. I conjured this rather bleak thought because they had previously won the Cup the day I was born. My spirit had become so entwined with the team that I thought there would be this mysterious connection of fates. I was born in the morning, and the Hawks defeated the Detroit Red Wings to win the Cup that night. I came into this world during a snowstorm in Oak Lawn. Hours later, Bobby Hull was carrying his first and only Cup around the Detroit Joe Lewis Arena. Therefore, my glory must end when the circle of life is completed.

Well it wasn't me, but my dad. The connection of his passing and the Blackhawks Cup was eerie. My dad was the reason we were such hockey crazed kids. My first time on ice in a competitive game was when I was six years old. I played goalie with no equipment. Fearless I guess. Our family had season tickets to the Blackhawks my entire life and some still do. He helped Don Borian as a chief promoter of a full size indoor hockey rink built in our hometown on the property of Homewood-Flossmoor High School. He was passionate about the game.

It's hard to know if the Blackhawks run in 2010 was resonating with him. By now there were grandchildren who had inherited the passion of the sport and followed every shot of our heroes. We tried to keep him abreast as his final illness overtook his spirit. Somehow, I believe my dad knew.

Thoughts of him hung in the rafters in Philadelphia as my son and I worked our way close to the ice surface for the post-game celebration. I had visions of my dad and how we might have climbed these plexiglass walls to join the new breed of Hawk heroes-Jonathan Toews, Duncan Keith and Patrick Kane. Though that was out of the question, we did celebrate with Chicago Bears star Peanut Tillman, a big Blackhawks' fan himself. For Tommy that was pretty cool. We banged on the Plexiglas as players paraded the Cup feet in front of us. A physical exclamation point on our evening.

It might make this memoir more engaging if I inserted a daring story of escape from the rugged home team fans as we attempted to leave the Wachovia Center. But it was eventless. The Flyers fans who remained in the stadium or were loitering outside were lamenting their latest heartbreak. They weren't looking to break our arms or legs. They were defeated for the sixth time in a row, and they received my empathy. Their sadness was palpable. Their defeat hung in the air as a reminder of the many times the Hawks had done the same to us in Chi-town. It enhanced my appreciation of the night's magnificence.

At this moment, I wished for them what I hoped for my Cub fan friends in 2005 after the Sox championship. That someday soon, they would have a night like this. It happened for my Cub fan friends, but not these Philly fans. I still feel for them today. They didn't beat me up or pelt my son with flying objects. They took their defeat with grace. For that, I am obliged.

The Blackhawks continued on a very successful five years of playoff triumphs and ridiculous finishes on their way to establishing themselves as the best team of the decade. Their next championship came in the wildest last minute in Final's history. In 17 seconds, the Blackhawks went from losing to the Boston Bruins in Game 6, thus forcing a decisive seventh game, to winning the Cup in the famed Boston Garden. The Hawks' bizarre scoring spree of two goals in less than half a minute set off another Chicago celebration. They had clinched their second Cup on the road, and across the Windy City, fans erupted. This time I did not go; however, my brother John finally made the trip and was present for an epic Finals game. I still smile at that thought.

I watched the game in Martin's Tap in Steger, Illinois. My friend Jimmy owned the bar. I witnessed the late two-goal barrage with a few others and celebrated with a dozen plus tipsy fans. It was a south suburban-style celebration.

Two years later, they brought the Cup home, literally. The Hawks' clincher, this time, came at the Chicago Stadium, where it should have been back in 1971. Several of my family members witnessed the ultimate game in person. Lord Stanley took his long-awaited ride on the shoulders of greats in the Madhouse. I watched from home with my family, fulfilled.

PERIOD 07

I would love to say it was the ascension of athletic height as a key talent evaluator that prevented me from having a professional hockey career. But the fact was I didn't want to work that hard, and oh yea, I lacked some serious talent. I loved the game and understood it, allowing me to perform above my skill level. In drills, I would not be the first or the fastest. My shot lacked speed and force though it was reasonably accurate. I had severe conditioning issues and struggled to last a shift longer than 20 seconds. In fact, I was the opposite of the adage, "Don't play sports to get in shape; get in shape to play sports."

I was the counter to all of that. I liked game day. Practice bored me. Drills? Forget about it. I lacked the humility to practice. Maybe a couple of warm-up shots at the goalie, and I was ready to go. Preparation? None. At the level I was playing, the results were adequate. I scored a lot in high school and eventually at a college club level and many late-night men's league games. My teams won more than we lost, and I never got hurt.

The highest level I played at was eight games for the nascent Texas A&M University (TAMU) club team—a team that didn't exist until a few fellow Aggies and myself willed it into being. I was a junior at the College Station campus when I noticed a flyer announcing a tryout and introductory practice for the TAMU lacrosse team. It was 1982. I had yet to learn what lacrosse was, though it sounded like a combination of basketball and hockey. So I went to the initial tryout. It was the first time I had ever seen a lacrosse stick. I wasn't alone.

About a dozen unruly boys on the cusp of manhood ran around cluelessly for about 90 minutes before the leader said, "Let's go to the bar to talk about the team." We all agreed and headed to the famed campus bar, perhaps one of the American college's most famous bars—The Dixie Chicken—then a spring chicken of a bar, but an institution now.

After a pitcher or two, the 10 seated around the table introduced themselves. I started by saying, "I'm Tom. I'm from Chicago, and I know nothing about lacrosse. I only came out today because I thought it would be like hockey."

The fella seated to my left spoke next.

"Hi, I'm Myles. I'm from Boston, and I know nothing about lacrosse. I thought it would be like hockey."

Like an AA meeting for forlorn hockey players, we went around the table. To a man, the story was the same. After we shared a laugh at our lacrosse ignorance, in unison, we said, "Let's start a hockey team!"

It was my first experience in community organizing. We had to build a team. There was a lot to it. It would be one thing to start an on-campus organization from scratch in any pursuit. There would be student committees to get approval and university officials to sign off on the school's logos, licensing, not to mention finances and fundraising. Add that to the formidable task of starting a hockey team in Texas in 1982.

My brother Dan (forefront) reacts to Konerko's slam heard around the Chi-town. Later named a Chicago Tribune Best Photo of the Year. Back Cover photo credit: E. Jason Wambsgans/Chicago Tribune/TCA

My brother John (brother Chris in background) finally share the thrill of holding the Stanley Cup with one of the Mt. Rushmore of Chicago coaches Joel Quenneville. Photo credit: Scott Dobrez

My son cheers along side the greatest takeaway machine in Bears' history Charles 'Peanut' Tillman as the Blackhawks celebrate their first Stanley Cup win in 49 years. Photo credit: author

The old scoreboard clock at the Chicago Stadium. Go ahead tell me how much time is left? Photo credit: Wikipedia

The memorial wall at Wrigley Field that became an outpouring of human connectedness after the first Cubs World Series win in over 100 years. My dad is remembered as 'Papa Bear' in yellow on wall. Photo Credit: Nick Dobrez

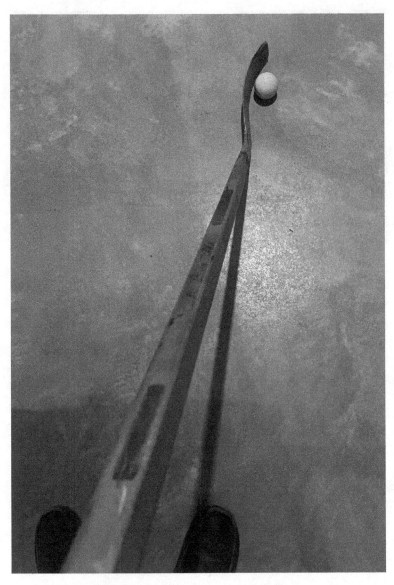

Bobby Hull's curved stick circa 1969 still in my brother's possession. A legion of youth burned their fingers trying to melt their own sticks to curve them with Bunsen burners. Photo credit: John Dobrez

There were plenty of obstacles to clear, like securing the most critical ingredient to any hockey team (or keg party): ice. Then it was sticks, followed by money, uniforms, well, you get the point. With little hockey infrastructure anywhere in the state, our challenge was even more foreboding. Our first team president, Steve Mathiason, navigated the university hierarchy, while Dirty Dave McDonald helped create team unity with car washing fundraisers. I pushed forward on the public relations front.

As a budding journalist for the school paper, *The Battalion*, I got a few stories planted about our progress. I made sure our introductory meetings were adequately promoted. That led to a groundswell of players of like minds and souls. The Canadian transplanted Anderson brothers joined the fray at one of our introductory meetings. With their network, we grew to a formable size of nearly 20 players looking for home ice.

We found a sheet of ice to practice 100 miles away from campus, or so we thought. The Sharpstown Ice Arena in Houston was one of the state's first rinks dedicated to hockey. We booked the Sharpstown rink for our first-ever practice. The team would caravan the two hours for a 90-minute training on a Saturday morning. That was the plan; however, we should have checked the weather.

The night before practice a lightning storm passed through the Houston suburb, destroying the rink's power system. The ice melted overnight. We didn't know until we got there. A setback? Indeed. Was it a team killer? Nope. With support from rink management, we reserved a few minutes for practicing at a shopping mall rink. The Galleria Mall opened its doors for us, and we conducted our first skate around on a less-than-official-size ice sheet with no nets. We were quite the anomaly for Houston's suburban shoppers that fine day.

After that abbreviated practice, we continued the search for ice and other equipment. In the Midwest, it's easy to find a selection of necessary equipment like tape, skate laces, and sticks. Not so much in Texas in the mid-1980s. There also was no Amazon to ship anywhere for free. We needed everything, but most of all, we needed sticks. As friends and family of teammates made plans to drive down for a campus visit from a northern state, we placed large stick orders. The family member, usually a dad, would load up the car with a trunkful of wooden implements and head to campus. We were grateful and treated their arrival like Christmas morning.

Stick shortage resolved, we continued our search for ice. We spent most of our first spring playing floor hockey in the now-demolished Deware Field House on campus. This led to another of my public relations coups when we had a photo published in the paper with the headline, "Beware In Deware!" The semester ended with little hope. We lacked equipment, uniforms, money, and teams to play. With a summer to get our act together, we resolved to make this happen. We laid out a plan for the semester break.

When we returned in the fall of 1982, we would continue our quest. We returned anew with more potential than ever. With the Sharpstown ice arena renovated, our "home" practice rink became our beloved go-to spot. It was the only time I enjoyed the practice. I didn't believe we would ever get to play an actual game.

Mathiason had secured university approval for uniforms and even a few dollars to help get them paid for and produced. The players returned from the summer break with equipment and additional supplies like tape and laces. There were more than enough sticks now. We were on a mission.

That mission culminated on the eve of Halloween in October 1982. We had scheduled a two-game series on the road against Tulane University in New Orleans. If nothing else, we had an excuse for a road trip to the adult Disney World-NOLA. For the trip down, Mathiason had commandeered a van from the university and drove the team's hockey bags and excess sticks to New Orleans. Five of us made the trip in style in my 1972 big-block 454 Chevy Caprice convertible. A vehicle for the ages that had surpassed 100,000 miles on its maiden voyage down to College Station three years earlier (with Dave aboard). It was a tad older but still a chick magnet of the highest rank. Anyone who has ever seen that car remembers it.

I took the Anderson brothers (Gordy, Joe, and Tom) along with Todd Steinweg down in the red beast early Saturday morning. We arrived and headed right for the rink to see if there was ice. There was. Game 1 was moments away. We passed the time at Pat Carberry's (my friend since first grade and a student at Tulane) house. As game time neared, we embarked to the rink and suited up. The puck drop was at 5:30 p.m.

Despite only three practices on actual ice and rarely with our complete team present, we skated our asses off. We were releasing the last eight months of pent-up energy. Like a campaign team that had been knocking on doors in unison for the cause, we all came together for a brief shining moment of our own. We had overcome numerous obstacles in building the impossible dream of an ice hockey team in Texas. We had a singular focus, and here we were, fulfilling our shared goal. Our last obstacle was the Green Wave of Tulane. They were the easiest part.

We cruised to a three-goal victory and celebrated in the locker room like we had clinched a Frozen Four invitation. Months of prep erupted in laughter of disbelief. Amongst the smell of sweat convalescing on ratty hockey equipment, we planned our celebration. We headed to Bourbon Street.

A group of misplaced Yankees from the north, who had found themselves on campus in the middle of Texas, had conspired to start an ice hockey team. These college students now found themselves victorious in that team's first-ever game. Strangers just ten months ago, they united into a working unit of cooperation and teamwork on and off the ice. Boys on the brink of manhood, some just approaching their 21st birthdate, were about to be set loose on America's craziest street. Oh, did I mention it was the Saturday before a Sunday Halloween?

The post-game is the definition of epic. For many of us, it was a night of many firsts. Our first team game, first win, first Pat O'Brien's hurricane, and first time seeing grown men piss on the major thoroughfare of a city. But I digress. It was a night of fable and myth. Still, it happened.

Besides providing years of storytelling, the night also led to another first. Our first loss. Those intelligent Tulane students had scheduled the second game of TAMU hockey history for Sunday at 8:00 a.m. We were a tad unprepared. As gallant of a battle as we could muster between vomiting on the bench and trying to stay awake, we couldn't keep up with the Green Wave. They shell-shocked us 9-6 in our second game ever. We couldn't have been happier.

On the drive back to College Station that Sunday afternoon, we were on the Atchafalaya Basin Bridge- a multi-mile expanse connecting New Orleans to Baton Rouge. It is an engineering marvel, suspended over the bayou for 10 miles with traffic only going one way. There are no shoulders on the road, and it is susceptible to significant traffic jams if something goes wrong. Something went wrong this day. A car accident closed the road with us somewhere between Tulane and Texas. We didn't care.

We set up a game of touch football amongst all the stopped vehicles who watched us with curiosity. I had a Duke football in my car. We played for an hour plus. When cars moved again, we called the game and jumped back in the convertible. Joe Anderson had the ball. His brother Gordie called for it while diving back into the car. Joe threw it. It came up short, and one bounced over the bridge into the Louisiana bayou. We all gasped. The passengers turned to me, knowing it was my cherished football. They had puppy eyes.

I laughed it off. "Fuck it. That ball will always be here to remind us that the Spirit of Aggieland lives in my brothers, who accomplished the un-accomplishable. Building a hockey team in Texas."

Or some bullshit like that. Forty years later, we all remember that football sailing over the railing and into our memory scapes.

Years before any professional NHL team called the state home, we embarked on the nearly impossible: starting a hockey team in Texas. It took us a little over seven months to play our first game. The machinations of the process taught me a great deal about grassroots efforts and how to get things done. It took energy, resilience, communication, and drive. A few guys and I took the leadership mantle and guided the team in its inaugural season. As attested at a recent weekend on the Texas A&M campus, we started something that has lasted. There is a sense of pride in building such a foundation.

In January 2022, the current TAMU team invited us to campus to recognize our feeble beginnings on the 40th anniversary of that faithful afternoon at the Dixie Chicken. It was the first time many of us had seen each other since that fabled first season ended in the spring of 1983. The specific details of the inaugural year became as slushy as ice before a Zamboni cleared the memories anew. We each recalled certain days, moments, jokes, and shots—most of them were the drinking kind. The game-to-game details slipped our minds. I could only confirm them via old copies of *The Battalion* newspapers in the online archives. However, the sense of accomplishment endured.

A few rag-tag misfits made something happen. The little team that could chugged up and down the ice. Today's Aggie hockey team is a rising star in the Western Collegiate Conference and draws a consistent fanbase to each game. They welcomed us on this chilly weekend with reverence and curiosity. We regaled them of the old days. They turned our little side project into something significant, hoping to become a sanction collegiate team sport. We follow the team with a sense of pride and accomplishment. Would someone else have started the team if we hadn't? No one knows. We know that a group of strangers from various upbringings came together and built something. Is it saving lives? No. Is it enhancing them? Absolutely.

From my raging youth shooting rubber pucks between the piano legs in our basement, thru college years of creating a team out of thin air to a night for the ages with my son in Philadelphia, hockey has provided moments of transcendence. In a powerful essay in *The Atlantic*, Arthur Brooks describes transcendence as "a sense of awe, a feeling of oneness with others or the divine, and a loss of the boundaries of space and time." That sounds like what I experienced on that Halloween Eve in New Orleans and on that June night in Philadelphia.

There have been other moments in the sport when similar feelings arose. As fans, we are searchers. We bond with others as we cheer from the stands, in the bars, and living rooms; through that, we seek purpose. We are part of something bigger than us: a community that needs us. We pray, we shout, and we are there for our club. It gives us meaning. It's near to religious belief—searching, community, and purpose. Sports and religion—these things are not unlike each other.

Chapter 3

When We All Danced With The Bulls

QTR 1

I was not in the arena for all the Chicago championships of my lifetime. In fact, I missed six of them over an eight-year span. It would have made this memoir all that more complete had I had a hurried story of my adventures to see the Michael Jordan show. I barely paid attention to the greatest dynasty Chicago ever assembled (the Bears of the 1940s notwithstanding).

The Bulls' run remains the peak of Chicago sports' finest decade. During the 1990s, the Cubs were the only team to miss the playoffs. The Hawks had a solid run, making the conference finals four times and advancing to the Cup final once (a spanking by Pittsburgh in 1992). The White Sox won the AL West division twice and, by many accounts, had the league's best team in 1994 when a strike cancelled the World Series. Even the Bears escaped mediocrity for a spell and won three playoff games, as much as they won in any decade since the 1940s. There was plenty to keep a Chicago sports fan occupied.

It was also a pretty spectacular run for the city of Chicago itself. Besides Jordan, we had Oprah Winfrey's rise, and a gentleman named Barack Obama won his first election to represent city dwellers in the Illinois statehouse. We rivaled Seattle as the alternative music capital as Wilco, Smashing Pumpkins, Eleventh Dream Day and Liz Phair rocked onto the music scene. Top chefs like Charlie Trotter and Rick Bayless were putting the city on the culinary map. Mayor Richard M. Daley cleaned the streets and put flowerpots on the sidewalks to host the Democratic National Convention. We were coming of a new age. A city on the rise.

But unlike the music, food, and shopping renaissances, the Bulls' championships didn't move me. During their awe-inspiring run to basketball immortality, I would be lucky to attend one regular season game a year at home. I remember taking each of my kids to one game during that spell. In a time frame where I went to scores of Sox, Bears, and Hawks games, I inexplicably missed the run of the decade in my city. We spent the early nineties raising kids. By 1994, we had three children and by decades end, we entered the teenage years filled with youth sports and menstrual cycles.

I did, however, benefit from a business relationship that afforded me ample opportunity to see the Bulls play their dreaded rivals in the Palace of Auburn Hills near Detroit. My client owned a skybox in the Palace, often inviting me to share it with my friends. We'd watch the game in style and then enjoy a post-game visit to the Windsor Ballet, providing unmatched entertainment at a favorable exchange rate. The Bulls/Piston rivalry during the 1990s was bloodletting. Controlled violence enhanced by athletic grace. Ten pugilists engaged in a ring 94 feet long and 50 feet wide. Each game was hand-to-hand combat, whether the season opener or Game 7 of the conference final. You didn't show up at those contests looking for love, for it had been lost.

The Bulls/Piston rivalry goes back to the mid-1970s. Detroit greats like Dave Bing and Bob Lanier would battle the Bulls in playoff series that are now forgotten. They rival the more known battles of the late 1980s and early 1990s. The Isiah Thomas–led Pistons, otherwise known as the "Bad Boys," who introduced the world to "the Jordan Rules"—an overly aggressive approach to the game engineered by Pistons' coach Chuck Daly. It worked, as the Pistons beat the Bulls in back-to-back conference finals on their way to two NBA Championships at the turn of the decade. The second of those finals in 1990 went seven games capped off by the infamous Scottie Pippen migraine.

From 1989 to 1991, The Bulls v. Pistons battles were the NBA. Over the three years, the combined playoff record of the two teams (not including games against each other) was 54-14. The Bulls beat the Pistons nine out of their 17 playoff tilts as the two teams won three NBA titles in a row (and 8 out of 10). To be a visitor to Detroit for some of those battles was an experience. Viewing the battlefield below from the pampered confines of a sky box suite made it even finer. As I commiserated with friends partaking in the free booze and poorly seasoned Italian beef sandwiches, man-to-man combat unfolded 60 feet below our vantage point. As we relaxed in cushy seats with ample leg and arm room, below us titans tangled in a raw exhibition of sport. Up at the suite level, the major confrontation was the smell of hot dogs over coming the scent of expensive perfume worn by the patrons. The basketball games were like football without pads. It was near my entire exposure to the dynastic Bulls.

Despite my indifference to pro basketball, I have had a couple of chance encounters with two of the game's biggest stars. I golfed with Toni Kukoč and played Pop-A-Shot with Scottie Pippen. The Kukoč match was prearranged; the Pippen encounter was a genuine brush with greatness.

I introduced the game of golf to my Croatian born friend, Augie Mimica. He invited me to join his fellow countryman for a round of his newfound love. We would play golf with Kukoč right after the Bulls won championship number four. What a delight to share 18 holes of camaraderie with a champion and a fellow Croatian. Despite being the bane of Pippen and Jordan's existence upon his arrival in Chicago, Kukoč proved his mettle with his stellar play. Named the league's best sixth man, he proved worthy in the clutch. Eventually, he won the minds, if not the hearts, of his fellow players who shunned him in the Olympics.

I took particular pride in Kukoč's career with the Bulls, primarily since he was Croatian. Growing up, I had little interaction with the vibrant Croatian community in Chicago. When asked in grammar school about my heritage, my response would illicit giggles. Often people would think I said 'creation,' since we were of no nationality of import. That all changed on September 10, 1976. I was fifteen years old and looking for an identity. On that fateful day, five "Fighters for Free Croatia" hijacked a TWA 727 headed to O'Hare Airport in Chicago. They were seeking independence for their territory from Yugoslavia. A few months later, Michael Bilandic would become Chicago's first Croatian mayor. Suddenly, it seemed we were all over the place.

This terrorist act had a strange, unifying impact on our family. My dad took a certain amount of pride in the attention the story was getting and had red t-shirts made for all of us that read in white letters "Free Croatia." I wore mine with significant pride to school. The recognition of our homeland began a journey of discovery for me. I became engrossed in studying my roots. I wanted to understand what was a Croatian. It's been a lifelong journey that has echoed through to my children.

When my dad passed away in early 2010, we paid homage to his passing with a voyage to our homeland. Thirty of his progeny headed to Dubrovnik as part of a cruise in the Adriatic Sea. I flew out early to spend a week in Croatia with my mother, wife, and children. The country along the sea had been crawling from the wreckage of a civil war that rocked the Baltic states in the early 1990s. Nearly two decades had passed since the fighting ceased, yet remnants of the war's vestiges remained. It was a solemn reminder of havoc caused when identity overcomes acceptance.

Part of our trip included a voyage to the birthplace of my grandfather, John Dobrez (known as Ivan in Croatia). My grandfather left Croatia at 11 in 1906. Our pilgrimage included a stop in the town of Dobreć. The hometown of our ancestors and origins of our surname. The pronunciation of the last letter ć in English is close to the sound of our letter 'z'. Thus the spelling change to our Americanized last name.

Inspired by pride of place, Croatia has become a cherished family identity. Cousins get the text messages going as Croatia takes the pitch in the FIFA World Cup. Each year, we try to go to St. Jerome in Chicago for their annual festival of all things Croatian. The pride bug passed on to my son, who choose Dubrovnik for his study abroad semester while a student at LSU in Baton Rouge.

For me to play 18 holes of golf with one of our homeland heroes was a special moment conjuring significant gratitude. Kukoč's golf game was, let's say, at a rookie level. He struck a few balls that may still be up in the air and he made some nice putts. His final score was dismal; however, he brushed it aside casually with, "Uh, my actual job is over." Indeed, it was. He was a champion. I beat him that day in strokes. I could not do that again. Once his engine ignited, Kukoč embraced the game with an athlete's mettle and became a dandy player. He'd crush me today.

The splendid documentary, *Once Brothers*, covers much of the turmoil Croatia went through in the 1990s. Part of the ESPN 30-on-30 series, the film, directed by Michael Tolajian, is the story of the Yugoslavian World Championship basketball team and its subsequent dissolution caused by political upheaval. It's a must-watch for any fan of sports as politics. Shortly after the premier of the show on ESPN, I had the pleasure of joining Kukoč for dinner. Kukoč shared his remembrances of those playing days with us at an informal dinner chat that became memorable. His demeanor was of one who had been in a war (literally) and came out with a

renewed perspective on life. He seemed able to compartmental-
ize life's trivialities after facing such cruel indignations as a junior
player. After sharing head-shaking stories of what it was like to
play basketball in Europe, he taught me a new perspective. He said,
"I had to make a free throw with fans screaming at me at Madison
Square Garden. People asked me if I was nervous. I say you should
be a 13-year-old playing in a foreign country as fans whack your
knees with sticks as you run down the sidelines."

He shared some hard-to-fathom anecdotes of gymnasiums
with the doors opened on the opponent's shooting side, allowing
the wind and snow to converge on the court. Home team advantage,
to be sure. Kukoč and his band of brothers survived many humil-
iations on their way to the European and World Championships
that shook up the basketball world, only to be sidetracked on their
way to the Olympics by political unrest that led to a civil war in the
country they were representing. Their success was an impetus for
the development of America's Dream Team.

A simple act during a post game celebration by Yugoslavian
team member Vlade Divac led to rapid dissention of the team's
unity. The players became flotsam of a movement out of their
control. The movie is a powerful testament, both tragic and inspir-
ing, of sport's ability to unite and divide. A genuine life and, unfortunately, death tale. In the Balkans, the team's accomplishments
are the sporting equivalent of the USA gold medal hockey team.
Their tale became tarnished when politics and sports boiled over.
The world has seen its share of sports used for political theater
since Hitler in the 1936 Olympics. It reached the nadir with the
1978 FIFA World Cup in Argentina and the US and Russia's subsequent boycotting of the Olympics in the 1980s. A decade later,
Kukoč's Yugoslavian basketball team became pawns in a brother
versus brother modern day civil war.

In the film, Dino Radja, a team member born a Croatian in
Split, says, "One side makes up the story of how they like it. One
side makes up stories of how they like it."

When these stories rooted in identity collided, conflict rose and friendships suffered. As Divac says, "Basketball was no longer important. We just wanted peace. Politicians used propaganda to fuel hate." The story's poignancy resonates and acts as a primer on how great things can fall apart fast. What the team went through was absurd. This group of young men had come together from disparate lands to become one of the world's finest sports units. Tribalism destroyed it. They all received harsh treatment from rival factions. It tore them apart as they prepared for their crowning moment– a chance at gold in the Barcelona Olympics. Banned from competition, the Yugolsavian team split up, leaving a fractured Croatian team to compete and win the silver medal after giving the first Dream Team all it could handle in the ultimate game.

Civil war cheated Kukoč and company out of world prominence, yet he and the others took life lessons from their hardships. Today, he is a successful father and businessman in America who has embraced life and its quirks. He understands what is truly important because he once had it taken from him. They learned hard lessons, lessons in stoicism.

The narrative arc of the film is a father, Vlade Divac, talking to his son. It's a real life drama of how sports can bring people together and how it can tear them apart. Kukoč admits that talking to his former teammate Divac during the turmoil became all too hard because of family bonds. He was told not to speak to him or he "would have a problem." Time helped healed some wounds, but the battle left scars. Divac returned to the capital of Croatia and visited the grave of his lost teammate, Dražen Petrović, a proud Croatian and sensational basketball player who lost his life in a car accident before Divac could make amends. The solemn moment released inner tensions that haunted Divac for years. He recalls the emotion as "a sadness I couldn't escape until now." In the end, sports redeemed. Brothers became united in the game and torn apart by it as well.

QTR ▦

My encounter with Pippen was much more hilarious. My friend Pat had set up his annual treat, securing two company seats for the traditional President's Day game—a Monday afternoon matinee. It was a Jordan retirement year. Pippen was the unabashed star of the team. On this day, however, he sucked, and he couldn't blame a migraine. He owned it. In one of Pippen's poorest showings in his Hall of Fame career, he scored 11 and fouled out. The Bulls suffered an unusual home loss. It was an off day.

Pat and I didn't really care. It was fun enough being at a mid-season game. It was early in the evening when the game ended, and we needed a beer. We headed to Bixby's in downtown Chicago. We sat at the bar with less than five other patrons. After all, it was early on a Monday evening after a long three-day weekend. As we chatted in the near-empty restaurant, the door swung open, and there appeared not one but four beautiful women dressed to the nines, as they say. Pat and I couldn't help but ogle them with jaws dropped. We couldn't believe our luck. A group of incredible-looking women just waltzed into the bar we were at? Then, he walked in behind them all.

Scottie Pippen entered the bar by lowering his head to fit inside the door frame. He glanced around and pointed to the booth just to his left. The women obliged and filled the red velvet semi-circle bench. Pat and I looked at each other. "It's Pippen!"

We laughed it off and ordered another drink. We might stay here awhile. With Pippen in the house, anything was possible. The two or three other bar rats didn't even notice his presence. We thought it was fantastic.

After another round arrived, Pat and I decided to play the Pop-A-Shot near the door. Pop-A-Shot is that crazy-ass indoor basketball shooting game where you get an allotted amount of time to make as many points as possible by sinking mini basketballs. The game is about 8 feet long, and the hoop is maybe

8 feet off the ground. Small balls return to the shooter via a tarp that rolls them back into your hands for rapid-fire shooting. The more shots you make, the more points you get, and the highest score wins. Now Pat and I are barely 11 feet combined in height with wing spans to match. The game presented a certain amount of challenge to us. We played a few rounds against each other, and then a person in the bar walked over to check in on us.

Hovering 12 inches over us, he said in a deep, bellowing voice, "You boys want to play for money?" As he said that, he pulled out a roll of cash four inches thick. It was all hundred-dollar bills. I'd say, conservatively, it was $5000 in cash. Pat and I looked at each other, amazed. At what, we weren't sure. Was it more insane that Scottie Pippen was challenging us to a basketball shootout or that he was brandishing $5000 in US Benjamins?

We mumbled something and then said, "Uh, well, we will play you, but how about for shots?"

Not sure where that came from, but Scottie loved it.

"Sure," he said. "This is how it's going to work. You two get a turn, and we will add your numbers together. Then I will shoot and beat your total. Losers buy."

"You're on!"

We did not do the math or worry if it was a fair bet. We should have thought about how much this might cost us. Or ask if we had to buy shots for his four fancy escorts. We just said, of course, we will take on Scottie Pippen in a basketball skill challenge. How could we lose?

Pat shot first and put up a respectable 18 points. I was next 17, one of my better runs. We had 35. "Good luck," we offered our opponent, who also happened to be a seven-time NBA All-Star and future Hall of Famer.

Pippen started the game. It was like art meets poetry meets grace meets athleticism. It was beautiful. Pippen's arm motions were like a ceiling fan getting up to full speed. He was dropping balls into the hoop with one hand while the other hand was readying the next one. It was a flying repetition of speed and agility, the likes I had never seen so close up. It was mastery. He scored 76 points.

Pat and I just laughed through the first tequila shot we had to pay for. We had witnessed greatness in a Pop-A-Shot game. We doubled down and asked for a rematch. He might have gotten lucky. We improved our numbers. And so did he. We lost again by at least 40 points. It was awe-inspiring to watch the ease at which his arms, hands, and eyes all coordinated to reach greatness. Though it was only a bar arcade game, the excellence was apparent. The skill level is on a whole different scale. Pip said he was hoping to score 100 in 20 seconds. We laughed with Scottie.

Near the end of our trouncing, I asked Scottie, "Why did you walk up to play with us? I mean, you play this sport for a living. Do you really need to get up here and play more basketball?"

"Well, uh, yea. Tonight, I need this. I didn't get my minutes in," he answered.

"I was going to tell you, you played a great game today, but I didn't because, well, you didn't," I said. As it left my mouth, I knew I might have been overstepping my bounds, but the tequila overruled my executive functioning skills at that point. Did I ruin this evening?

Pippen just roared. He laughed his ass off, bought us the next round, introduced his girls to us, and signed our ticket stubs from the game. Pat and I somehow made it home.

The next day, Pat called me from his office. "It happened, right?" he asked.

"You mean the Pippen thing?"

"Yea," Pat said, "I'm here in my office, and I'm telling everyone we played Pop-A-Shot with Scottie Pippen, and no one believes me."

"Pat, you have the ticket."

"What ticket?'

"Remember? He signed our tickets," I reminded him.

"That's right. I forgot about that. Hold on; I think I have it in my wallet. I do. Gotta go. I need to show my co-workers," he said.

As he hung up, I laughed to myself. What a night. Pippen was great, the night was memorable, and it heightened my appreciation for all things Scottie Pippen. Don't tell me he was soft. If he was, he was soft in the heart. He appeared that night as a kind gentleman who loved to have fun. A brilliant specimen of an athlete, he was a staunch champion, the likes of which Chicago has rarely seen. Don't bad mouth my man.

Pippen was a cool guy with a funny voice. Sometimes, he cherished his role as Michael Jordan's second fiddle. When he didn't, he tended to take his frustrations out in the media. It's understandable. He played over 1000 games for the Bulls and is the only player in basketball history to win an Olympic gold medal and an NBA championship, twice, in the same year. They named him one of the 50 Greatest Players in NBA history, yet most Chicagoans think "migraine" when they hear his name.

Scottie Pippen was the perfect Robin to Jordan's Batman. A physical specimen who knew how to finish. Defenses could not deny his drives to the hoop. It took guts, strength, and fortitude to do what Pippen did for the Bulls. Jerry Krause, the oft-ridiculed villain of *The Last Dance*, traded up in the 1987 draft to grab Pippen, a relatively unknown commodity playing for Central Arkansas—a second-division school. For this alone, Krause deserves accolades. The Bulls' incredible six titles in eight seasons still rank as a premier dynasty in any sport. Pippen was a significant cog in the success. Yet, a few acts of defiance, stupidity, insecure behavior and one lousy decision tarnish his legacy.

Like any of us, Pippen made a few mistakes in his career. Then, some tough breaks clouded his record. In the 1989 conference final, Bad Boy extraordinaire Bill Laimbeer lambasted Pippen with an errant elbow after a rebound. The scene is hard to digest. As Pippen drops to the floor, the play continues. Pippen remains prone as the

Bulls make a defensive stop and return to the offensive zone, where Pippen still lies in agony. The referee slides Pippen off the court in the middle of the action. Eventually, time is called. Pippen left the game, never to return. The Bulls lost the series that day. In another elimination game, he experienced a blinding migraine. He scored only two points. The Bulls lost the game and the series. Pippen's reputation turned sour. Fans and media depicted him as soft. They were also comparing him to the greatest of all time. It's hard for me to accept that Pippen was soft. It was unfortunate. But really, you think he didn't want to play?

Pippen's reputation suffered again when he refused to play in a 1994 playoff game. With less than two seconds left in the game and the Bulls in an offensive timeout, head coach Phil Jackson drew up a play that called for the Bull's rookie Toni Kukoč to take the game-winning shot. Pippen refused to go back into the game. Kukoč made the shot, and the Bulls won. Pippen lost respect. He still stands by his decision years later, though few can see his point. In one interview, he hinted at Jackson's decisions as racist. This was not a bright scene in Pippen's complicated presence in Chicago sports.

The truth is Scottie Pippen is human, which is to say he is no Michael Jordan. There can only be one Batman. Jordan's excellence overshadowed his own failings—gambling, womanizing, and being a challenging teammate. Pippen had no room for error as a second fiddle, and his public pronouncements often made things worse. Ridicule built rancor in him. His malevolence tore at his legacy unfairly. Meanwhile, Jordan simply dismissed the negative charges against him, and the media obliged. Pippen was easy pickings, so they dug.

Most of Pippen's transgressions aligned with the response most of us would have had. Yet, they angered the masses. We expect greatness in our idols, not mere mortal behavior. Except for the 1.8 seconds he refused to play, Pippen's most significant crimes were off the court, usually in interviews. (Arrested once for an actual crime of illegally possessing a handgun.) It was his need for acceptance that drove much of his lapses. He felt under appreciated. Some times the emotions that had been boiling under the surface released and it was caustic. Pippen moved on after one of his explosions. He would return to the floor and continue to excel year after year. He just had to get a load off his chest.

The magnitude of his discretions is minimal. He hurt no one. According to *The Last Dance*, he did not cause unrest in the locker room. He just wanted to be seen. Except for one ill-advised decision on the court, Pippen delivered. It was a privilege getting my clock cleaned by him in Pop-A-Shot on a Monday night in the city of tall shoulders. That night, I hung with two of the most towering shoulders the town ever had—the two of Pippen's that helped carry the Bulls to six titles and a decade of enjoyment.

Pippen's career is one of the finest in all of Chicago sports history. Six titles, All-Star MVP, and over 18,000 points while playing alongside one of the most epic scorers the game has ever seen; Pippen needs no explaining. Scottie rocks in the annals of the best the city has ever seen, and I rocked it with him for one night.

QTR ▓

The first professional basketball game I saw was a blowout. The Harlem Globetrotters destroyed the lowly Washington Generals. I can't remember the score; however, I know the Globetrotters won. They wouldn't lose a game for the next three decades. My exposure to the game as entertainment intrigued me. I couldn't understand why this team of tricky, talented ballers never won the NBA championship. Then again, it was hard even to know who won the NBA championship back then.

I had little exposure to the NBA until Michael Jordan arrived on the scene. There is not a single game I remember attending with my dad. The early greats of Bulls' history, like Chet "The Jet" Walker and Bob "Butterbean" Love, played in front of sparse crowds smaller than most high school football games in Chicagoland. We only seemed to pay attention to professional basketball because they had cool names like Dr. J, and the guy I became enamored with, Wes Unseld. He just sounded cool.

The NBA of the late 1960s received minimal press or live TV coverage. Newspapers were the primary news source, and they rarely covered the game. The front page of the daily paper (and sometimes twice daily newspaper) dictated what we were to care about and who we were to admire and shower with accolades. Basketball was nowhere to be found. In the sports pages, it was all about baseball and players like Billy Williams and Ernie Banks. It was like basketball didn't exist. It was even more pronounced in my inner circle.

During my youth, so-called sports fans insisted basketball, even at the professional level, was not equal to other sports. Though we played the game in Catholic league grammar school and on our backyard court, the game at other levels had minimal appeal. We'd mostly ignored the professional game because finding information on the league took a lot of work. There also may have been a tinge of sports-ism involved.

In my woken state, I have tried to come to terms with the disdain of the game many around me shared. If it was institutional racism, the data does not correlate. The rise of the NBA in popularity coincided with the 1979 NCAA Finals, pitting Earvin Johnson against Larry Bird. This was three years after the ABA merged with the NBA, significantly increasing the percentage of Black players. The pro players in my adolescence were majority white, and nobody cared about the game then. It was during the late 1970s that the game saw an influx of African Americans. That coincided with the league's increasing popularity. Yet, in my sphere, the game hardly existed. I listened on the radio as the Bulls reached the conference finals in 1975. For most of us, they were an afterthought. We just wanted a team from Chicago to win something.

It was as if basketball was a culture and not a sport. Then it became a sport via Magic's Lakers and Jordan's Bulls. The culture of basketball was something that didn't connect with me. I eventually learned to appreciate its athleticism and came to reckon with it as a sport, though race remains an enigma when discussing the game. Some still judge a team's potential by its racial makeup. To this day, people still comment about how many Blacks and whites are on the court while watching a game on TV. It seems innocent, though it is at the very least stereotyping.

The Kareem Abdul-Jabbar scene in the movie, *Airplane*, exemplifies the attitude. A boy visiting the plane's cockpit suggests that, according to the white kid's dad, Abdul-Jabbar is lazy on defense. Abdul-Jabbar, who was playing a character named Roger Murdock, breaks out of character to become himself and schools the youngster on what it takes to play professional basketball. It was a lesson for anyone who did not consider basketball a sport. It was a prevalent thought in my neighborhood. An anti-basketball sentiment persisted all around me. If it wasn't racism, it was undoubtedly its close cousin, unconscious bias rooted in ignorance.

My apathy for the professional game made little sense. I was a crazed youth who did any physical activity, including playing entire games in my backyard, where I would be the leading scorer, the defensive tackler, and even the referee. It would enthrall me in my imaginary stadium of the backyard. Years later, my mom would tell me how she would watch me from the kitchen window, amused and entertained, as I played entire games alone. As the quarterback, I would let the ball fly, run down the field, toss the ball again to simulate its flight pattern into my hands as the receiver. With ball caught, I'd juke the imaginary tackler while plunging for the goal line, which was the clearly defined marker between the tree and the post of the deck at the back of the house. In the end zone of my fantasy, I'd quickly pop up to see the referee signal the touchdown with two arms raised. I stepped around where I had fallen to where the referee would have been on the play and made the two-arm extended signal. It might have been the first time in sports that the same player threw a touchdown pass, caught a touchdown pass, and signaled a touchdown on the same play. I did the same on the cement basketball court my dad installed in our backyard. Hitting dozens of game winning shots in games of my imagination.

I look back now at the world that surrounded and influenced me to ignore the game of professional basketball. Football, baseball, and hockey were staples of my sports' loving youth. I'd read newspaper accounts of games and devoured *Sports Illustrated's* provocative writings on the big three sports. For basketball, there was a noticeable void of interest. Many of my fellow sports enthusiast friends also disliked the game for unwarranted reasons.

It wasn't like my surroundings were fertile grounds for such prejudice, either. My beloved community of Flossmoor was on the leading edge of integration in the mid-1970s and remains a beacon of diversity to this day. One of the earliest Black residents of our community was a gentleman who arrived in town via a Rolls Royce. Muhammad Ali, the one time and soon to be again and again heavyweight boxing champion of the world, was also my neighbor.

Flossmoor is a gem of a community established in the south suburbs of Chicago in 1924. Initially organized around the sport of golf, it has thrived because of its openness to individuals regardless of race, creed, or sexual persuasion. It remains welcoming to residents of all faiths and color. Our neighborhood was diverse before people knew it was a thing and there is no doubt Ali helped make it that way.

None of the Ali biographies I have read mention our town of Flossmoor by name. An unfortunate omission, but the fact remains: Ali, his wife, his ex-wife and mother all had homes in our little village. One proud mention occurred in the opening sentence of an article in the November 18, 1974 Vol 2 No. 21 edition of the nascent *People* magazine with John Wayne and Kathryn Hepburn on the cover.

"It is dusk on Bobolink Road in Flossmoor, Ill as a Rolls-Royce moves quietly up to a plain, raised ranch house where Muhammad Ali is…" opens the story by Ronald B. Scott. Scott chronicles the champ's suburban exile after he regained the heavyweight championship by defeating George Foreman in Zaire (now the Democratic Republic of the Congo). Ali had not lost the title but had it taken from him years earlier by US authorities for his refusal to serve in the US war in Vietnam.

Ali had purchased a few houses in the nine-block subdivision known as Heather Hill. With its castle like turrets at the subdivision's entrance and finely manicured lawns, Heather Hill was a dream enclave served by a highly regarded high school - Homewood-Flossmoor. It was one of the first neighborhoods to integrate. And one of the first to cross the racial divide was The Greatest.

Once, in the spring of 1973, after Ali had his jaw broken by Ken Norton and was considering retiring, he came to our town looking for some peace. That spring afternoon was full of sunshine and warmth. The maples were coming into bloom and the scent of almond flower filled the breezy air. I was doing what I usually did on nice days. Played sports. Today it was Home Run Derby in the front yard, pitching against the garage. On my team was "Butts" Marty McCabe. We were playing against Mark "Squinchy" Dore and Jim "Bob" Whitting, all members of the nickname hall of fame. As we were getting ready to start another inning, one of the largest vehicles I had ever seen pulled up to the stop sign in front of our house on Sunset Avenue. The Champ was in town.

An arrival like his was the analog version of a post going viral. It was the early 1970s. Every kid in the neighborhood was playing outside, and when a limousine enters the town, everyone knew it. Nowadays, you may not even notice a limo cruising through your neighborhood thinking someone is getting a ride to the airport or its prom night, but back then a limousine did not make its way down these hamlet streets too often. We dropped our mitts and ran through the backyards of our suburban neighbors to Bob-O-Link Road (*People* magazine misspelled it). We knew where that limo was going. When we arrived on his street, kids were everywhere. He had a way of attracting a crowd, whether a remote African village or our little town in Chicago's south suburbs.

Ali exited the limo as his entourage stood guard. We watched him from the bushes. He visited with a few of the other kids who were playing across the street and invited them into the house! That's right. As Ali exited his vehicle, he waved the kids over and eventually encouraged them to come in to get to know the family.

Ali's appearance in the neighborhood was an event every time it happened. The next time I set eyes on him was at his daughter's eighth grade graduation. A relative was also graduating and therefore, I could feign interest while really getting a look at The Champ. They moved the event to the larger high school gymnasium in anticipation of his presence. When I entered, I looked around. The calmness of the crowd assured me he hadn't arrived yet. As the pomp and circumstance began in his absence, it crossed my mind that he might not be coming. So I ditched the graduation and headed out of the gym towards my car. And then I saw it again. A limousine parked in the most peculiar spot behind the gym. It had to be Ali, so I inspected.

I broached the limo and its shaded windows. I was hoping for any kind of peak of the passenger, thinking it could be The Greatest. As I crept closer to the car, in a less than conspicuous way, the rear window rolled down. I froze.

"Hey" a voice rang out from inside.

"Yea, Hi," I responded, I think.

The rest of the conversation has disappeared from memory. I know I spoke with him and he with me. I know we joked about the crowd in the gymnasium awaiting his arrival and I know, or at least I hope I said congratulations on your daughter's graduation, but that too is foggy. The certainty of seeing him, the window coming down and the voice greeting me was what I remember. And will never forget.

Years later, I would consume stories of Ali wherever I could. Via documentaries, biographies, Hollywood movies. All of them reiterated different versions but similar stories of Ali's gregariousness. Ali loved to chat and make people feel welcome. He was the people's champ. Making you feel respected regardless of age or status, he made you feel you mattered. Throughout his life, he'd engage with random strangers, whether outside his wife's home in Flossmoor or on the streets of Zaire. Ali was accessible.

His presence on my TV screen and in my family room was shocking. A black man was rising in a white world positively. My fondness for Ali grew watching his verbal battles with Howard Cosell on ABC's *Wide World of Sports* and the grainy, celluloid, footage of the Super 8 films my dad would buy for us to watch the heavyweight fights months after they were over and we already knew the outcomes. My respect grew deeper as I followed his career during that timeless interval when he was the Pied Piper for scores of kids who called Heather Hill their neighborhood.

Ali was the future and the present. He was ground breaking. Everybody loved him. A black man that integrated so much around the world, opened our eyes on a micro-level in our humble village. Though his stance as a conscientious objector to the Vietnam War riled my veteran dad, Ali's omnipresence on our televisions and in our town helped him understand. My dad was not so rigid in his stances that he couldn't change his opinion. Ali was more than the World Champion; he was our neighbor. My dad made peace with that. He cried like all of us when Ali lit the Olympic torch in Atlanta in 1996.

Ali's presence in our suburban community was a harboring of things to come. Black, Asian, Jewish families flocked to Flossmoor during Ali's residence. As America's eyes were opening, so was our little town. Today it sits as a model of what the future could look like. Welcoming and connected to each other. To me, he was a hero. His skin color was a non-factor. I was color blinded by his greatness and kindness. I look back and consider those true brushes with the Greatest and try to square it with my anti-basketball sentiment. It doesn't square.

The anti-basketball sentiment unraveled in 1979. The Larry Bird/Magic Johnson NCAA Finals had much to do with that. But think about it. It was as symbolic as it came: white against Black. It would take a unique Black person to overcome the sentiment. He had to smile a lot; he did. Magic beat Bird on that famed March night as the 1970s ended. But he won more than a game. He won the hearts and minds of America. Magic's ascension into the culture of America coincided with so much awareness of his chosen sport and the acceptance of the Black race—for the time being.

The Magic/Bird championship game opened many of our eyes to the game's grandeur. As the sport entered our living rooms regularly, prejudices melted away. Familiarity with the intricacies of the game improved our appreciation, and with it, heightened our attention. I still lacked commitment, though. I don't remember attending a Bulls game until the Michael Jordan era, and I have yet to make one playoff game, let alone a championship final. In the post-Jordan age, I still struggle to concentrate on a game for longer than 10 minutes.

In fairness, it would be too simplistic to say my lack of interest in the NBA was ultimately racist. The NBA was a second-rate league full of white guys during my impressionable youth. The Bulls were born after I was. There was zippo media coverage, and even though the Bulls had some compelling players during my teenage years, we hardly knew what they were up to.

Bulls were always second fiddle to the Blackhawks, who themselves were already third or fourth rate to the other Chicago sports franchises. The best thing the two teams had going for them were some pretty badass uniforms. The Bulls and Blackhawks ruled their leagues with solid unis. Meanwhile, my forlorn White Sox tried every design imaginable, even paying an ode to 16-inch

softball—a genuine Chicago sports original—by wearing shorts
one year. It took some time before landing on their classic silver
and black look today. In any year, they still paled to the Blackhawks'
Indian head and the Bulls' raging color scheme.

I had been a casual basketball fan at every level, meaning I
was a bandwagon jumper. I followed my high school team down
to the state's Elite Eight when my soon-to-be brother-in-law was
part of a third-place team. Years later, I returned with my children
to watch our shared high school—Homewood Flossmoor—make
one better than the 1985 squad with a second-place finish. Unless
one of my kids is playing, I didn't make a regular season game. I
coached the game more as a father spending time with his children
than as an aspirant for a better gig. I could take or leave the game.

Like many, March Madness brings me all the basketball I
need. I enjoyed the thrill of 'amateurs' laying it all on the line for
what will be the last game of their careers. Buzzer beaters became
a thing. The attraction breeds community, or is it the community
that generates the interest? Everyone fills out a bracket regardless
of knowledge. The country unites over three weekends. We share
a conversation. We laugh, console, and admire as a unit. Then it's
over. We go back to our things. (I've been to a Final Four, and it's
the same experience from your TV rooms, except you are much
farther away in the arena. Stay home is my suggestion.) It's a distraction we all partake in, like turkey on Thanksgiving. We can have
a dialogue with strangers. It's a good thing for our American souls.

QTR 4

The Bulls are a solid franchise co-owned by White Sox owner Jerry
Reinsdorf. They made the playoffs in nine of their first 11 years of
existence; however, they didn't genuinely excel until a particular
draft pick from North Carolina arrived. Much like Magic Johnson
leading the Los Angeles Lakers at the beginning of the 1980s, the

Bulls went to new heights behind Michael Jordan by the end of the 1990s. That's when I started paying a little more attention because you had no other choice.

My first Jordan game, in person, was all I needed to see the light. He was on an insane run of nine straight games of scoring 40 or more points in December 1986. We had tickets to witness the record-breaker. Michael failed miserably. He scored a season-low 11 points against Milwaukee. Yet, I became a convert. Watching Jordan in person, even from the rafters, was an epiphany.

My basketball knowledge is limited. Playing in Catholic league games in grammar school and brawls on our backyard court amounted to my entire education in the sport. My appreciation of the skills it took to succeed was even more rudimentary. When I watched the budding Jordan on TV, he would make everything seem like a simple play. The overzealous announcers would shout a series of onomatopoeias to explain their wonder. I sat there, unimpressed. It didn't look like he had done all that much. When I saw MJ in person, it all changed. Despite his failure to break the record the first night I saw him in person, he excelled like no athlete I'd seen before.

Witnessing his grace in person was like visiting the mountaintop. On one particular play, Jordan, on the court's defensive end, would block a shot and secure it in his 11-inch hands. From there, he would lead the fast break down the floor. A few seconds later, he would tomahawk dunk the ball on the opposite end of the court in a singular gesture of inhuman fluidness. He would do this many times per game. When I'd see that on my TV, my tepid response was, "It was ok." From my limited perspective and no reference, he only moved about 20 inches—the width of my TV—during the play. It looked like a decent effort.

When I saw it in person, it challenged my grasp of physical space and athleticism. Jordan's feat of leaping high enough to make the block, which again, on my TV, was only an inch or two, was a high jump of nearly 40 inches when seen in person.

His subsequent rush down the court was not a mere two feet, as displayed on my pixels at home, but a lengthy full-court drive of over 60 feet. The slam was an aerial projection of 15 feet to a 10-foot rim explosion. In person, it was awe-inspiring. The magnitude of his feat amazed me. All for two points in a game that had hundreds. It was the sheer athleticism that caught me off guard. I couldn't comprehend crossing the court that fast, let alone performing two significant leaping feats on both ends. And, by the way, five guys on the other team were trying to prevent him from doing any of this. My appreciation for his level of greatness skyrocketed during that game—a match Jordan would probably rather forget for his dismal performance. Despite his disappointment, he converted a casual follower. It moved me to recognize his worth, and my admiration for him and his first chosen sport started to grow.

With Michael Jordan, it was hard to ignore the game. Like an opioid that cures chronic pain, Jordan's antics provided insulin to the Chicago sports scene and professional basketball. His epic campaigns in the NBA were one of those moments in time. It became more than a good run; it became an era—the Michael Jordan era. His ridiculous run of six championships over eight years remains an incomparable feat. I didn't see one of them. Not a single home playoff game during the ring years. I skipped the parades as well. I am not sure why. Could I call myself a Chicago fan?

My fondest recollection of their championships was their first. It's one of the most impactful memories aligned with sports I carry—and what a fond memory it is. Because far more than any championship, by any team, in any sport, I won that famed day: June 12, 1991. My wife and I were the real champions as we welcomed the second child to our family, Caroline Joan, named after her cherished grandmother. Of all the championships I watched, whether in person or on TV, it is the only one I remember the exact date. I can tell you the Sox didn't stop believing in October 2005, the Bears cruised to Super Bowl glory in January 1986, and the Hawks owned the 2010s. Though saying without peeking at Wikipedia, the exact date of those moments would be a wild guess. The Bulls' first victory is a date that lives 'in-family.' Apologies to FDR.

The reality was I could take or leave the Bulls' glory. With their first title, my memory starts and ends with the birth of my middle child. Without the recent reminder of *The Last Dance* documentary, I would be hard-pressed to name the opponents in the series. Though a quick Google check confirms they beat the Lakers with Scottie Pippen leading all scorers in Game 5, I remember John Paxson making just about every shot he took. I recall my wife saying hours after her labor, "Go out and celebrate with Bill Hogan at Bob & Clara's."

The Bulls of the '90s brought us together in living rooms around Chicagoland. My extended family embraced the team. My mother-in-law exhibited a tremendous amount of enthusiasm over the sport and the Bulls' run. I profess joy in watching and discussing games with her, as did her family. In those moments, sports as a familiar bond exhibited its pull. Three generations shared those evenings of jocular conversations about the merit of Jordan's uncanny ability to deliver in clutch moments or Rodman's insane ability to excel on the boards. There was an instant connection you could make with an aunt you didn't see that often or a distant friend you came across in the grocery store. We all knew every detail of this team as they roared into our lives. You could rely on the Bulls like the summer equinox. As the school year ended, they began. The bandwagon backed up to every living room in Chicagoland.

Family affairs became mini-sports radio mockeries. Grandma always had uncanny insights, and the brothers-in-law chimed in with their ill-informed demagoguery. We knew Phil Jackson was a Zen master, even if we were unsure what a Zen master was. The sisters commented on the team's personalities while the grandchildren were soaking in the banter of people in love communicating without screaming at each other. The joy of dinner was heightened with focused conversations about the merits of five men running the triangle offense. Family united around a shared enemy—the Bulls' next opponent.

My interest rose during the decade for its calming effect on internal and external tensions. They were a conversation piece, a light we all could bask under. It was simpler time when political factions existed, though they didn't ruin Thanksgiving dinners. We had the great unifier of a great sports team in our midst. We could all agree on them, even if we couldn't agree on the color of Dennis Rodman's hair.

The second championship caught me in the city. We had a client dinner planned for a few weeks, and it fell on the night the Bulls clinched. The evening started with a meal fit for a king at Chicago Chop House. We sat dumbfounded as the Bulls looked lackluster and fell behind by 15. We thought at least we could enjoy our dinner. Then the 4th quarter started, and the genius of Phil Jackson went on display. He sat Jordan and left Pippen as the only starter on the court. The bench rose up and closed the gap to three. Enter the Sandman. A well-rested Jordan seized two late defensive steals as the Bulls eliminated Clyde Drexler and the Portland Trail Blazers. As the city-wide celebration kicked off, we joined the revelers in the streets. It was my first night in the anarchy of a city gone bonkers.

Cities erupt on championship nights with unbridled enthusiasm. It's a reflection of the goodness of society when an event triggers such massive happiness. Because who doesn't like a fabulous party? The energy is palpable. It permeates through the populace and manifests itself in communal joy.

This is best displayed by a video posted on Facebook shortly after the Kansas Jayhawks won the 2022 NCAA basketball national championship. The videographer was standing outside a bar in Lawrence, KS (home of KU). He's at the top of a hill looking down the town's main drag. It is still. He pans his smartphone right to peer over a wooden fence sealing in an unknown number of bar patrons. Their attention is on the large screen broadcasting the ultimate game. On the recording, you hear Jim Nance calling the last seconds of the Jayhawks' victory over the North Carolina Tar Heels for their fourth title in school history.

Then, the controlled madness begins.

Taking a cue from the spirits of triumph thundering down from somewhere in the far reaches of the universe, the students begin an orderly yet rapid emptying of the bar. Many are still determining their destination. They are being pulled by something, a magnetic force of exultation, demanding they move towards it. It being everyone else. They are pouring out of the bar and swaying into a frenzy with their fellow undergrads. Like water pouring into a bucket, they are seeking their own level.

There is pure ecstasy in their voices which are not speaking words as much as guttural projections. Some are jumping frog-like into the night. Others are in an accelerated walk, some hand-in-hand. None are obtuse to their fellow man. They are synching together in a cloud of humanity on the city's main drag—Massachusetts Street. Tonight, it will live up to its nickname—Mass Street. It is now a street of Mass, human mass. The camera catches scores of kids pouring out of doors into the river of delight. The exile erupts as bars along the route empty of patrons. Fireworks brighten the night sky. There's no end to the young adults congregating. It's the dawning of jubilation.

The social media post is a stunning account of the madness and beauty of crowds. It's exhilarating to watch, no matter who you cheer for. The shared merriment mesmerizes you. You catch the revelers up to something good. It exudes positive energy from its togetherness. These kids had so much joy they needed the world to see it. They also needed to share it. That's the thing about happiness. Once you have it, you want everyone to have it. It's the high you can't wait to share. My Sox title experiences felt the same way. I just wanted to shout it from the rooftops. My energy was of such profound goodness it had to be distributed broadly. This is what rapture is. Religions speak of such overpowering greatness that it cannot be contained.

Souls who experience the moment find the glory enhanced with the boundless sharing of its rewards. It is what we seek.

Those revelers on that March night in Lawrence were like hordes of others in towns and cities when champions were crowned in America. It was what we got caught up in as we exited the Chicago Chop House after the Bulls secured ring number two. All of us wanted to join the band. A night you can't forget. As it's happening, you experience great pleasure. The moment's significance pulls at you and makes you relish it. Because of its scope, it is close to nirvana. Fellow citizens surround you; you know not their name, care not their race, nor fret their threat. They are like you—happy as shit. You want to engage with it and with all.

This is the greatness of sports in America. They can bring a lifetime of disappointment and then satisfaction in a heartbeat. The bounce of a ball controls the strings of joy. The revelers at the University of Kansas had done very little to make that night happen. They cheered and jeered throughout the season. They made outrageous comments like how they would make a better coach than Bill Self. Some criticized the ref or made derogatory comments about the teenager playing for the other team. Yet, their team overcame, so they celebrated. There is an energy in those crowds. The video from the Kansas night struck me because it was an on-the-ground view of how such events metastases. The controlled elation of the students was one of, "We are all in this together. WE did it."

The Bulls' celebration that night was the first time I had been in the mix. It was madness, but it was safe. It was joyous but, honestly, it was impossible to get a drink! Which was ok, because you didn't need one. The night's inebriation occurred as the throngs gathered in the city's streets. The energy was bespoke upon each one of us. It was rapture.

These championship nights are exceptional from all points of view. Whether from your home TV, the city streets or in the arena, you want to celebrate good times. And there is always room on the bandwagon and I thank the Bulls and their fans for letting me on.

You Are The Pride and Joy of Illinois

Every year, there are enthusiastic preseason predictions of the potential greatness for every team. And each year, you ignore past disappointments and become a staunch believer again. Then, one year, you turn out right. The 1985 football season was just that in Chicago. And if we didn't know it all along, the players certainly did.

There was a measured anticipation that this would be a special season. In fact, it might even be super, but since no Chicago Bears team had ever made the Super Bowl, it was in doubt until it wasn't. It was a long time coming, and it's been a long time hence. Going into the season, we thought the Bears might be good. We didn't know they would be *this* good. Did we think they'd be the best ever? How could you?

Like most Chicago teams, the Bears of the late 1970s and early 1980s were not very good. Despite that, attending their games was always fun, no matter the score or weather. Tickets were scarce but available, especially for late-season games when Bears' playoff hopes had already vanished. Thus was the case when the Hogan family invited me to attend a season finale. It was the end of another forgettable year for the Bears, but it would be a memorable day with some devoted fanatics. I borrowed my father's RV, and Bill Hogan and I enhanced one of his family's sacred traditions: tailgating.

Tailgating is a whole thing that I must attest I am not very good at (Read my story about the White Sox World Series Game 1 if you have any doubt). But some Bears fans take their tailgate more seriously than the game, and some give it equal billing. That was the Hogans.

The elder Hogans were five brothers sharing season tickets since the 1940s. One brother was a season ticket holder for the Chicago Cardinals when they shared the city limelight. Their family of fans grew to include cousins and, eventually, grandkids. There have been few games in the last 60 years where the Hogan seats sat empty. Some times it could get challenging. Certain games provoked a series of frantic Sunday morning phone calls to figure out who was going and how they would get the tickets physically in their hands. In the end, this one family was emblematic of hundreds like them throughout the city. Their devotion to their team is multigenerational and unconditional.

Bill and I planned to meet his uncles at TR's Bar in Oak Lawn at 7:00 a.m. I tooled the RV around the front of the South Side landmark saloon and strolled into an already raucous environment. After a Bloody Mary and a few beers, the Hogan gentlemen wished to investigate the RV. They wanted to be sure that I, and the ride, were worthy. They couldn't believe their luck.

Though the weather forecast said it to be 10 degrees in the old Soldier Field that day and a wind chill in the negatives, these Hogan men would arrive in style. It was the Ritz Carlton of tailgating, and they were royalty. They were attending with me, which made me feel privileged. They gave me street cred. The feeling was mutual, and they let me know it—respect amongst our comrades in arms.

When we arrived near Soldier Field, the parking attendants instructed us to drive around the stadium since we had an RV. As we traversed the traffic, we were continually told to move ever closer to the entrance gates. As we got closer and closer, the gentlemen in the back of the bus began hooting and hollering. The RV was finally told to stop about 20 yards from the gate to the entrance. It was historical and hysterical. Bill and I could only laugh at our dumb luck, and the elder Hogans looked at me with even more dumbfounded respect. I got lucky for showing up. We laughed and prepared the tailgate. Most of which we spent in the RV because now it was brutally cold outside on the lakefront. This didn't bother us. What good is an RV if you stand outside it?

A few minutes before kickoff, the Hogan uncles left the warm confines of the RV and headed to their seats in the north end zone where they had been holding court for decades. Bill and I had other seats, a little closer to the 50. We downed another beer and waited until after kickoff before waltzing into the old Soldier Field.

Bill and I watched a quarter of the game from our frigid seats and then looked at each other and said, "A tv, warmth, and free beers in the RV?" So we left the meaningless game and took up residence in the camper for the final three quarters. To our amazement, the elder uncles stayed in their ridiculously cold seats for hours to watch the last game of another dismal season. They rode it out. They were the guys I would travel to New Orleans for when my good fortune dropped a Super Bowl ticket in my hand.

The 1985 Bears season is almost beyond explanation. Besides the team's dominance on the field, there were enough sideshow escapades to fill a couple of seasons of a situational comedy. Off the field, the characters were memes before the term entered popular culture. It was a pre-social media storm that would have dented the Internet had it existed. From Jim McMahon's antics and fiery Coach Mike Ditka, to the rabid fans caricatured on *Saturday Night Live*, this was the team America loved like *The Simpsons*. This real

TV family played football better than anyone on Sundays with a cast of stars, including the best ever to play the game.

The Chicago sports landscape is full of talented players who never got to host the banner of champion in their respective leagues. The names of Ernie Banks, Jeremy Roenick, Dick Butkus, Gale Sayers, Bob Love, Chet Walker, and Carlton Fisk—all Chicago greats who never won a championship. It would have been a shame had Walter Payton's name stayed on that list.

Payton was a hero of remarkable talent and moral character. I'm sure he had some issues at home, but he carried a franchise on his back for a dozen years. His early seasons saw some of the shittiest teams the Bears have ever assembled. Yet, Number 34 continued to produce Pro Bowl numbers. Everyone on the field and in the stands knew he was getting the ball. Off the field, be it on a post-game report or at the Chicago Auto Show as an endorser, his demeanor and ladylike high-pitched voice carried the day. Never has a nickname been more appropriate: "Sweetness."

I had the honor of making his acquaintance once. I was a snotty teenager at the time, and he managed to impress the cynical me during his Chicago Auto Show appearance. He was not much bigger in stature than I was, and yet he carried himself with dignity and grace. Throughout the event, he was smiling, saying "Hi" to everyone, and asking personal questions of each of us as we received an autograph and photo. He made me feel important. Everyone who ever met him feels the same. He and I were the only two people on Earth for that brief encounter. Walter is the greatest ever. Period.

Payton's statistical line is like a straight line going up. Every year, his numbers improved. In his first year under Coach Mike Ditka, the Bears were 3-6 (strike-shortened season). He was a leading rusher, and in 1984, the season before the big one, he passed Jim Brown for the most yards in NFL history. Now, he was leading a team to the Super Bowl.

The Super moment struck Bears fans at the same time. After disposing of the New York Giants 21-0 in the first round, the Bears faced the Los Angeles Rams in the NFC Championship. A game, in Coach Ditka's words as the Smiths (Rams) against the Grabowskis (Bears). The Bears led by 17 when a light snow began to fall over Soldier Field, creating a snow globe effect. Linebacker Wilbur Marshall recovered a Rams' fumble and raced 52 yards for a defensive score. His run was magical. We all knew it then.

Chicago went bonkers. The lions in front of the Art Institute sported Bears' helmets. They converted highway signs overnight to read 'Super Bowl Bound.' I know this because my good friend Dave stole one that was about 20 feet long. TV newscasts went 24/7 with information about the Bears. The team released a music video (earlier in the season) played by radio stations and TV shows non-stop. Every time a team member farted, news stations carried the sound bite. And everyone wanted to go to New Orleans.

There were a few ways to get a ticket to the game. Win the season ticket holder lottery, purchase on the black market for thousands, or a miracle. Seeing none of these in my future, I was comfortable missing this event. I scheduled a Super Bowl party at the house we were renting as newlyweds in Elmhurst. We were expecting a few dozen friends and family. I looked forward to enjoying the game in our little abode. Then, a phone call came.

I had been working for a media firm in Chicago. The firm was a broker for radio stations across the country. Each day, we interacted with clients from around the United States. On this day, one of those clients offered a miracle. On the Wednesday before Super Bowl Sunday, as the business day was ending, Greg Jankowski in my office received a call from one of our clients in Washington state. He had won two tickets to the game in the NFL lottery and couldn't make it and wanted to know if we were interested? Interested? Is a flower interested in the sunshine and rain?

Greg's resounding "Yes" resulted in a visit to my office, where he dropped the bomb. He was getting the two tickets overnighted and wanted me to go with him. How did this happen? I had only been working at this firm for a few months. In that short time, I befriended Greg, but for him to walk in to offer me a Super Bowl ticket was madness. I said, "Yes." Then we had to figure everything else out.

There were the usual logistics to figure out—plane tickets, lodging, a planned Super Bowl party I was to host, and a newlywed wife. Who was what? Just going to understand? We had married less than three months earlier.

Internet surfing was not a thing in 1986. You had to rely on your fingers to dial and dial. Painstaking phone calls to airlines and Amtrak, Hiltons, Hyatts, travel agents, and anything I could think of. I was working it. All flights to New Orleans sold out. Amtrak had seats, but the travel times were inconvenient. The solution? Fly to Houston and drive over. We could make sales calls with our Texas clients and slide on back home on Monday. There was no problem with Houston. I was heading there in 48 hours.

My thoughts turned to my wife Edie. She was working in the city then, and we commuted together. I would pick her up in our overpriced status symbol Saab and make our way out to the western suburbs through the crawling traffic to our rental house. This day, I was cautious as I broached the subject. She understood as a best friend would. Though she didn't entirely give a 100% blessing, it was enough assurance that I'd be welcomed back home the following Monday.

She didn't think about canceling the Super Bowl party. She was going through with or without me there. Ah, marriage! The right person can mean so much in one's life. I was lucky, and I knew it in more ways than one. Wives may not always understand, but friends do. And when your wife is your best friend, you are blessed. Blessed to be married to her and to be going to New Orleans, where I would represent my family and the thousands of other fans, like the Hogan uncles, whose passion I was bringing to NOLA.

Many felt the Bears were acting overconfident. You think? The team released the "Super Bowl Shuffle" video seven weeks before the championship. They had clinched nothing at the time. But what makes the video so enjoyable, besides Walter Payton's sweet vocalizing, is they lived up to the hype. Teams can show swagger as they attempt to force their opponents to lose focus. Eventually, they will need to show up. That's what this team had. The moxie. They could blow their horns and have the verve to back it up. There would be no denying this team.

McMahon spent the week distracting the attention from his teammates and putting it solely on himself. He mooned an aerial camera and allegedly partied into the wee hours. All season long, he was the mad focus of the media, from his goofy and imaginative headbands to the audacity to call out the commissioner; McMahon was changing the game forever.

All season long, McMahon knew what he was doing. He was a new kind of athlete before social media created scores of them; the Punky QB got on the nerves of league administrators because he refused to comply. He was the dawning of a new era of professional athlete.

McMahon was a rebel from a tight-ass school in Utah— Brigham Young. Can you imagine his years at the Mormon institution? He was supposed to have sworn off alcohol, swearing, and premarital sex and committed to wearing superman underwear. (NPR's Scott Simon later reported that McMahon wisely never signed the campus honor pledge, thereby relieving school officials of the need to suspend him.) McMahon did what he pleased and then threw six touchdown passes in a bowl game before most football fans knew it was even legal to throw six TDs in a game.

They called him the Punky QB, the nickname he gave himself in the "Shuffle" music video. He was punk, not punky, rad, not radical. Smooth around the edges. He knew what he was doing. Confidence can do that for you. McMahon knew what leadership looked like. He bestowed the role on himself when he acted the way he did. When a game was in hand, he flaunted for the sideline cameras. Football broadcasts were becoming competitive, and networks introduced more entertaining announcers. The game was moving closer to Hollywood in its production values and needed stars. McMahon knew that. He upset some of the old guards for sure. In doing so, he gave birth to a new generation of NFL fans. I like to see the change in male and female numbers watching football games before and after these 1985 Bears.

All the players carried such an air that they were impossible to ignore. They became national celebrities. It was hard not to see a Bears' player in every commercial. Refrigerator Perry, a freak of nature at the time, was selling what else, but refrigerators. McMahon sold everything; even the offensive line was getting in the act. Who can name an entire offensive line? Yet, here were Jay Hilgenberg, Tom Thayer, Mark Bortz, Keith Van Horne, and Jimbo Covert becoming household names. This team had already entered the national consciousness and still had a game to play. A loss in this game would have made all of them laughingstocks.

This 1985 Bears team laid it all on the line from the opening week. Their candid responses in post-game interviews were borderline cocky. Their off-the-field antics added to their entertainment value while setting them up for a grand fall. It would have been an embarrassment if they lost. Somehow, they knew they wouldn't.

Our Houston flight and drive over to New Orleans was how you like them, uneventful. A few clients of ours from Boston had set us up in rooms in their rental house. A magnanimous gesture. From there, Greg and I headed to Bourbon Street to join the pre-game of a lifetime. We worked our way through the revelers, pounded a few Pat O'Brien hurricanes, and listened to offers for our tickets. The asking price on the street was enormous. Today, paying two thousand dollars for a Super Bowl ticket is common. In 1985, the face value was $75, and tickets on the streets of New Orleans were pushing $3000. It was tempting.

Scams were everywhere, and there was a legitimate fear that you might get taken and/or arrested. In that light, we didn't even have our tickets with us. We laughed at some offers and took comfort in knowing we had a golden ticket to Wonka's Chocolate Factory, otherwise known as the Louisiana Superdome.

A little something about the Superdome in New Orleans: First, New Orleans is the perfect town for a Super Bowl. It offers many opportunities to run amok without worrying about the law. Stay safe, keep to yourself, and don't take any glassware on the streets. Pretty easy in the big easy. And, oh yea, try the Hurricanes despite them having little alcohol and lots of sweeteners. The Superdome has a storied history from its prominent role during the catastrophic Hurricane Katrina to hosting special sports moments like college basketball's Final Fours and seven Super Bowls. The size of the Dome is hard to fathom. It's large from the outside but massive on the inside. You can fit three of the world's first indoor stadium—the Houston Astrodome—inside the Superdome. There are nosebleed seats, and then there are those in the Superdome. They make your eyes bleed. Greg and I entered the stadium at the 300 level and walked up dozens of rows to find our seats. Once there, we searched for the oxygen tanks before settling in for the Bears' first Super Bowl.

Spoiler alert. The Bears crushed the Patriots in the end, but that's not how things started. Lost in all the madness surrounding the '85 Bears is that their most significant victory was a come-from-behind win. Only four previous times had a team come from behind to win the big game. The Patriots' lead was 3-0, which happened one minute into the game.[3] To us Bears' fans, and there were a lot of us in the Dome that day, the game's first offensive series was an ominous sign. A deflating feeling passed through the arena when Walton Payton, yes, that Walter Payton, fumbled on

---

3   The Patriots' opening drive field goal was the fastest score in Super Bowl history. A record that would last until the next Super Bowl I attended some 22 years later. That's when a stud named Devin Hester took back the opening kickoff against the Colts.

his first carry. He lost the football, and the Pats jumped on it. Do you believe in omens? Only when they come true.

SECOND QUARTER

In Chicago, we are big on omens. Not one of the five Chicago professional sports teams had won a championship in over 20 years (a pre-Super Bowl era NFL title for the Bears in 1963). The city of Chicago had just come off one of the most played bloopers in sports' TV history. The Game 6 muff of a lazy ground ball by Cubs' first baseman Leon Durham. That inexplicable error triggered a Padres' rally that led to the shocking loss in the National League Championship Series three months before the Bears' Super Bowl XX appearance. Durham's botch of a routine ground ball deprived Chicago fans of a championship again. It had become another symbol of Chicago's futility. (With the stink of the Cubs' demise still in our collective consciousness, I drew up a poster board sign for the Super Bowl broadcast that read, "Don't Send A Cub to Do a Bear's Job." Clever, eh?)

At the time of Payton's miscue, a hush went over the Bears' loyalists in the Dome. Were we watching another Chicago team disintegrate on the big stage? Would Payton's fumble become one of the most disappointing moments in Chicago sports history? (Jim McMahon would admit it was his fault.) High hopes were dashed. This fumble had an aura to it, but the Bears refused to abide by any curse. In the opening series, Buddy Ryan's defense did what they did, keeping the Pats from gaining a yard. Though we fell behind by three points after the field goal, we felt we dodged a bullet and had plenty of time to overcome. A TD there by the Patriots might have changed things. We don't know, of course. Despite what Cubs fans claim, we know that there are no such things as omens in sports.

Cubs fans and their media hordes have been blaming off-the-field antics for their ineptness for years. The biggest folktale in

Chicago sports may have been the 1969 team—a team I loved and could name every position player still to this day. They took their fanbase through an unprecedented collapse in the season's last weeks. They blamed their demise on a black cat. Years later, a die-hard fan took the blame for their complete evaporation against the Marlins in Game 6. (Please repent if you ever used Bartman's name in vain.) Cubs' media blamed Gatorade for Durham's error. That's what losers do. They blame outside influences that have nothing physically to do with the outcome.

Reexamine the Bartman case. The Cubs were on their way to a clinching victory and needed seven outs. A fan who attended the game alone touched a foul ball heading for the stands, as only a genuine fan might. The reaction of the Cubs' left fielder was so over the top that it impacted the entire team. Moisés Alou's baby wail went on for a few crazy moments. The Cubs had a Hall of Fame manager in the dugout sitting on his hands (Dusty Baker) and a rookie pitcher on the mound (Mark Pryor). As confusion reigned in the park and tensions rose, the manager did nothing. Baker didn't leave the dugout to calm his pitcher or team. He didn't instruct his 20-year-old on the mound to forget it and concentrate on the next pitch. He sat there without a word, and the announcers said nothing about his inaction.

Not to worry, the next pitch was a routine ground ball double play that would end the inning with no damage done. Except the shortstop missed the ball. Check it out. A perfect double play ball to end what was not even a rally yet skirted through Alex Gonzalez's leg under his Gatorade-free mitt. This was worse than Durham's snafu. There was no explanation for it. He flat-out missed it. The floodgates opened, and the Cubs lost the game. But they still were alive in the playoff. And oh yea, Dusty Baker did nothing after the missed double play either. Except for brood in the dugout. It was all Bartman's fault.

The reason the Cubs' lost was not a nerdy fan who did what most every human at a ballpark would do in that circumstance, catching a ball hit right to you. This blame game is a genuine issue for losers unwilling to face their shortcomings. Everyone wants a straightforward explanation for the unexplainable. It's how conspiracy theories start. When your mind can't wrap itself around a phenomenon, it seeks simple answers. A way for your brain to rest on a story as flawed as it may be. Bartman's actions on this night had little to do with the game's outcome. Cubs' fans and players were seeking a simple account of their fall. It was embarrassing and rude. Like the world of media politics and Americans' crazed passions on both sides of the political fence, everyone is seeking easy simplifications. They create a conspiracy to explain it all away. And they usually pick a scapegoat. Heck, there once was a time when Cub fans even scapegoated an actual goat.

Reality is usually much more nuanced. The Cubs blew that game and then a Game 7 lead as well the next day. In that game, the Cubs' starting pitcher hit a home run, yet they failed to clinch at home for the second night in a row. And you blame a fan? Bartman went into hiding for the next 20 years.

The Bears had a choice as well. They could get worked up over their leader dropping the ball on the first play on the biggest stage of his career or go out and kick some ass. You know what the Bears did. The defense controlled the line of scrimmage the way an ocean wave flows over a sandcastle. The Patriots stood at less than zero in yards gained in the first half. The Pat's starter, Tony Eason, did not complete a single pass in the game. They removed him for Steve Grogan, who saw most of the game sitting on his ass in the backfield. The Bears tallied seven sacks—a record still intact.

It was a performance that set them up for a glorious future, a team remembered by more than just rabid Chicago fans. This team would etch its place in the memory banks of football fans everywhere. They are the '85 Bears. Their devastating performance on the biggest stage cemented their legacy. They stepped up. You might say they had confidence in their confidence.

The second half of the game was like men amongst boys. We were actually afraid for the Patriots. It was a sandblasting. The Fridge tried to throw a pass, the defense scored, and a defensive player (Richard Dent) won the MVP. If you look up the word shellacking in Wikipedia, you might see a video of this game.

Other Super Bowl teams have eclipsed the records set that day, but never with this team's style. Their coaches (particularly Ditka and defensive coordinator, the much beloved Buddy Ryan) were leaders of men on similar missions. They both hold their place in Chicago lore. Their line coach Dick Stanfel is in the Hall of Fame, plus five starters. It was a team built to win over and over. It didn't. But on this Sunday in January 1986, the stars aligned. I saw history from the 400 level of the world's largest indoor sporting facility. Did the folks at my home, enjoying a husband-less party hosted by my divine wife, have a better view of the game? Yes. Did they see replay after replay of the ridiculous trouncing? Yes. Would they trade seats with me? Yes.

The rest of the day was just high fives and "I can't believe it" looks from the hordes of navy and orange-clad partisans. After a record-setting 21-point third quarter, the last quarter was an exhibition. Watching it was like a parade, a coronation of the team that would live in Chicago history. It's the team you tell your grandchildren about—the perfect balance of offense and defense. A near-perfect record during the regular season, symbolically diffused by the team they were chasing (the Dolphins) for football immortality—a Chicago champion in football and our hearts.

There would be restaurants, car dealerships, radio shows and even street names changed for this team. They acted like misfits, but they were a perfect fit. Each player played his role, and each coach got the most out of what he had. As a fan, you can look and say, "How did it all fall apart?" Why didn't they repeat, go on a Steelers-like roll, and win three, four, and five in a row? They were young and built to last before the free agency purge. Couldn't they keep their act together for at least another SB victory? How about just another appearance at the big dance?

After this blaze of glory, this team more or less underachieved. The following two years saw surprising defeats in the NFC play-offs, and the next trip to the big show was two decades away. Meanwhile, the Patriots, a team wholly destroyed in their debut on the biggest stage, rebounded for four more visits to the Super Bowl before the Bears returned. No one would have taken that bet on January 27, 1986.

No one cares about what could have been. Bears fans rarely harbor the fact that there should have been a couple more trophies bearing the name of the team's founder in the showroom. No, this team captured the imagination. They superseded any thoughts of what a champion looks like or how to measure success. The Bears defensive leader Mike Singletary had set the standards for the defense - No yards gained rushing, no yards gained passing, and no points. Singletary's statement that this Bears' team was looking for a 0-0-0 performance is a remarkable statement of purpose. And they nearly delivered on the game's biggest stage.

They went into a recording studio with the balls and best intentions (raising money for Chicago's needy) and declared their future. Nominated for a Grammy for their efforts, they somehow lost out to Prince for "Kiss" in the R&B Best performance by a band or duo. Was Prince a band or a duo? But that's an essay for another book. Strangely enough, that same Prince that rained on the Bears' Grammy hopes would also pour "Purple Rain" down on the fans in Dolphin Stadium at the next Super Bowl the Bears played at.

Fans remember this 1985 team as the pinnacle of athletic teams. They do not shame them for their inability to repeat. The Chicago fan demands effort first and success later. If you succeed, we cheer. If you look like buffoons, we will boo. It is a fan's prerog-ative, after all. To the young and old who gathered around their TVs on that January day, to the crazies who spent thousands of dollars on a ducat to be there in person, to the fortunate few who had manna drop from heaven into their hands at the office on a Wednesday afternoon, we tip a glass of beer for the Bears. We were champions, and we will always have Super Bowl Twenty. Damn, it would be nice to get another one, and we almost did. Once.

THIRD QUARTER

Since that SB appearance, the Bears have mired in the muck. The three years following the SB showed a team on the decline. Early exits and players' disgruntlement won the day. Injuries to McMahon and an abundance of linebackers who could not get enough playing time submarined the team's hopes. Ditka went from master motivator to hot head, trying to steal all the limelight. Buddy Ryan left in the perfect definition of the Peter Principle; meanwhile, the McCaskeys drew the purse strings in, and the Bears wallowed for years. Then the Bears drafted a kid out of Florida.

Selected on April 26, 2003, Rex Daniel Grossman became the 22nd overall pick of the draft. Bears fans have misplaced anger and grief over that pick. Lost on many is the fact that Grossman was the Bears' second pick of that round. GM Jerry Angelo went with Michael Haynes with the 14th overall. No, not that Mike Haynes, the Hall of Famer who played for the Raiders, but professional also-ran Michael Haynes. A defensive end out of Penn State who was out of football the year after Bears' Super Bowl 41 appearance.

Grossman was the fourth QB drafted in the first round after Carson Palmer, Byron Leftwich, and Kyle Boller. The Bears desperately needed a QB. The Bears had eight players, including Brian Urlacher, attempt a pass in the previous season. Jim Miller and Chris Chandler split most of the starts. To snag Grossman was a coup. The genuine mistake occurred with the first pick. The Bears had three of the first 35 picks after their miserable 4-12 campaign in 2002. It was just a terrible year to have such fortune. The next quarterback taken after Grossman was 66 picks later—a bench warmer named Dave Ragone. Only one Hall of Famer has come out of the 2003 draft class, the Steelers' Troy Polamalu, selected two picks after the Bears took Haynes. No one remembers that breach of duty by Bears' management. Grossman became the quarterback of the future by default—a lot in life that led the Bears to the Super Bowl. What more could he do?

Today, the mere mention of his name makes Bears fans cringe. Yet, Grossman led an over-achieving offense to the big stage. Miller's unexpected decline led to Grossman's selection. The Bears had developed a very serviceable QB in the Michigan State graduate who led the team to the playoffs in 2001. Then Hugh Douglas hit Miller, and he never recovered. The Bears' Angelo needed to reassess his signal caller situation. The downside of Grossman? He was injury prone.

Grossman's knee went out in his rookie year. In year two, he broke his ankle. After missing the bulk of the season, he started the team's last two regular season games, leading them to victories (including one over the dreaded Packers) and a playoff berth. I attended that Packer victory with Bill Hogan and his son, my godson, Shane. In the post game celebration we sang a new version of the classic '80's song by The Fixx. It wasn't zero but "we were saved by Grossman." In his first playoff game, Sexy Rexy struggled, and the Bears fell flat to a Carolina Panthers team at their peak. That experience would pay dividends in his third season. It also was an indicator of what we had in Number 8.

There seemed to be two sides to Rex Grossman. One was a superb decision-maker with NFL-caliber abilities and a laser arm. We could better refer to the other guy as Gross, man. His 2006 season was as symbolic of that as any. In September, he was the NFC Player of the Month. In Week 6, he fumbled twice and threw four interceptions in the infamous Monday night game in Arizona. A game followed by the tirade from the Cardinals' head coach Dennis Green who, in his post-game interview, imparted,

"The Bears are who we thought they were!" That was the wild quote Bears fans latched on to as our rallying cry by declaring, "We are who we think we are!" The funniest lines, however, came after that when Green bellowed, "You wanna crown 'em then their ass." Whatever that means, we got the point.

Where Grossman may have burned his standing with Bears' diehards was when the "gross man" showed up against the Packers in the last game of the season. Grossman's passing rating was 0.0 for the game. (No "Saved by Grossman" here.) The game had no bearing on the season's standings, and Grossman said he didn't prepare for it because it was "meaningless." No match against the Packers is truly meaningless, I guess. In today's NFL, it would be unusual for the starter to even play in a game with no impact on the standings or playoff positions. To Grossman's detractors, it was one more straw.

Grossman led the Bears to two playoff wins on Soldier Field. The second was a brotherly celebration for me as many family members attended the 39-14 Grossman-led blowout in the NFC Championship game over the Saints. The tailgate after the game was the real deal. Celebratory fans hung out in the Waldron Deck lot of Soldier Field for nearly two hours, reveling in the chilly night air and shouting, "We are who we thought we were!"

We were the holders of the George S. Halas Trophy and a date with the Colts in Super Bowl number forty-one. The Bears v. Colts Super Bowl came after 20 years of stumbling and bumbling Bears teams. Yet, Grossman remains an enigma of a terrible memory for Bears fans. I want to save Grossman's reputation.

For now, the Bears Nation was taking a road trip to south Florida. Unlike SB20, this Super Bowl would be a family affair for me. The Bears, behind an '85-type defense and Sexy Rexy, had advanced to the ship, and we kept our fingers crossed for our dance card. As season ticket holders of eight tickets, we thought we had a decent shot at the lottery. I have no proof, but the Bears' system was not very transparent, and I can't believe there was not some hanky panky involved, this being Chicago and all. We lost the lottery but not our enthusiasm to attend. I knew tickets would surface because of my previous experience at Chicago's championships. I booked the family for Ft. Myers and at least a roof over our heads at my parents' Florida home, two hours from the SB site in Miami. At least we were in the same state.

With two weeks to plan this one, we were perhaps a little overconfident that we'd get in. My goal this time was to get all of us in. My wife and three kids. The tickets would cost the same for five people, regardless of age. We hooked up with my brothers, sister, brother-in-law, and their kids. We spent most of the week looking for tickets. One of the most significant changes for us scalpers since the last Super Bowl the Bears played in was online access to the secondary market. There were still a few scams, but most of the time, you could be sure the tickets were legit. The problem was the price. SB tickets go high at the beginning of the two-week window as soon as the two teams are determined. They get low and go up right before game time and then down again, closer to kickoff, as sellers and buyers realize the deadline is upon them. It's essential to time the market. In baseball, season ticket holders own their tickets and negotiate their direct sales. With the NFL Super Bowl, the league holds all the marbles, and tickets have a once-in-a-lifetime feel; thus, pricing goes up, up, and up.

We scoured the Internet for a week and were uncomfortable with the prices. We sought freebies, direct ticket purchases from friends, or another business miracle. Nothing. We had a few decent price options go awry, as most ticket holders were well aware of the value of the ducats. Peyton Manning and the Indianapolis fans were seeking their first ring, and the Bears were the Bears. This matchup also had historical implications, as two African American head coaches (Lovie Smith and Tony Dungy) would face each other on the field for professional football's biggest prize. This hadn't happened before and hasn't happened again. In fact, in a diversity program gone back ass, it would be impossible to believe that 15 years later, there is only one Black coach, Pittsburgh's Mike Tomlin.

The typical way ticket prices rose and fell failed to materialize as high demand, and short supply remained. We still headed to the game. We drove out to Miami early SB Sunday. Our adventure called for a drive back after the game to stay in Ft. Myer's hotel since Mom and Dad's place was a little oversold with most of their offspring in town for the game. The day started nice weather-wise. We found a decent parking spot around the stadium and, with thousands of dollars in hand, began the ticket search. Lots of communicating with the brothers. Where they were, what prices they saw, and what they will commit. The market refused to move. We would make forays into the parking lot, searching and growing more desperate by the minute. The little offerings we found were still too steep. Offers were considered and eventually denied. No one was budging from their prices, and no one was buying at the prices. The marketplace couldn't find a price point everyone was happy with.

I always looked at the scalper game as the perfect example of economic market theory. The established price is when demand meets supply. If there are a lot of tickets available for the game, the price subsequently decreases. If, like The Masters, where tickets remain scarce, the price stays elevated. The key is the marketplace itself. Where are the tickets exchanged? Where is the intersection of buyers and sellers? When we approached Anaheim Stadium for the Sox World Series, tickets were readily available since Angels fans were looking to cash out. Ticket sellers were standing on the street a good mile away from the stadium. They wanted to grab any buyers before they got closer and realized that half the stadium was up for sale.

It can be like the feeling you get when you buy a new car. Leading up to your purchase, you feel like your car is unique, and there are a few on the street. Then you purchase one, and it seems like every other car is the same as yours. It's a bit of a mind game. The same goes for ticket scalping. If you are looking, you can find ducats. That doesn't mean you will buy, and its possible prices may be prohibitive. There is little wrong with getting near a stadium with cash, deciding on your purchase price, and not finding it. Then take that money you had already considered gone, plop it down in a bar or restaurant, and spend a good portion of that cash on a sumptuous meal while watching the game. The effort matters.

Another approach is the Grateful Dead strategy—look for a miracle. If you find yourself anywhere near the Will Call or stadium ticket office on game day, do yourself a favor and go up to the sales-clerk and ask if anything is available. Many games are "Sold Out," yet tickets miraculously come up for sale. Tickets released close to the start time get sent to the box office for sale. This happens at rock concerts all the time. The band and management typically set aside dozens of tickets for a show for friends, family, groupies they met in the last city, and so on. They usually will hang on to those tickets until maybe an hour or two before show time. More than once, I have found tickets to a sold-out event at the ticket window for face value, and they are usually excellent seats.

The next best tactic is to find someone who doesn't care. Find a guy that looks like he has never done this before. The guy with that faraway look. He had a couple of buddies screw him and drop out of coming to the game, and he just wants to get in the game and maybe break even. That's the guy you want to buy from. Treat him nicely, though, because you will probably sit next to him at the game. Offer him a beer in the stadium for dropping his price. The ticket has no value to him. That's what you want in a seller. Many times, guys like these are such good fans that they give the ticket away. This has happened to me more than once as well. If you want a miracle, you must look for it and accept it.

Like when I was scheduled to join my brother and his family at a sold-out Wilco concert during their heyday in Chicago. My brother had purchased six tickets, months in advance, of the show date. We were denied admission when we presented them to the ticket scanner that Saturday night of the show. The tickets he had were for the Friday show. Shit, out of luck, as they say. Our emotions went from sadness to hilarity in a moment. The screw-up was just too funny. Once his mistake was realized, we needed to scramble to get tickets. Being that there were six of us, it would be challenging. My first instinct was to check the box office—no luck. We then scattered amongst the crowd working their way into the venue, looking for anything. My nephews scored three reasonably priced tickets together—a miracle in itself. My brother found two for his wife and himself.

Meanwhile, I was not having much luck. My lovely sister-in-law, however, was another story. She was standing alone when a man approached her and asked if she was looking for a ticket. She said yes. The guy offered up one to her free of charge—a tenth-row, dead-center seat. The guy told her he had a friend in the band and he couldn't find anyone to go with him. He told her to enjoy the show and that he'd see her inside. Boy, was he taken back when I showed up in that seat next to him. Since my brother had already secured his two tickets, I ended up with the band friend's extra, given to my sister-in-law. A miracle indeed at no charge.

The next phase in the great ticket hunt is to look for guys with cell phones running back and forth like crazy. These are the professionals. They are simply working for the margins and don't need to make a killing, though they'd like to. Their goal is to make a few dollars more than they paid. If a seat costs them $75, they want at least $90 but will settle for anything over $80. They also usually have many seating options to choose from. They will start by offering you their hard-to-sell seats. You know—the nose bleeds. But deep in their pockets, they possess good seats. You can negotiate a price first and then upgrade the ticket. It's best to start by asking him what he wants for his best ticket and figure out the market from there.

Scalping has become a lot trickier game with mobile phones. Apps can sell and deliver your tickets right up to the start of the game. It has become electronic and ultra-responsive. So often, you don't really need to work your way around the stadium peripheral, seeking the marketplace. For buyers, there are few deals on the apps. You will pay service fees etc. The seller is a robot. He has set the price and has left the virtual room (puppy eyes on your Face ID don't work either).

The online market is elastic, so keep checking. Because of a business trip, I was stuck with a couple extra seats for a Bears game. I had put the tickets up at a reasonable price 48 hours before the game. They didn't move. Boarding the plane, I was in a something-or-nothing position. I lowered my price significantly. The game started as I was in the air. My tickets were sold and distributed to the buyer. That's a few bucks in my pocket I wasn't expecting, and someone I'll never meet had great seats at a ridiculous price for an NFL game. The ticket game has changed. Most of my years of scalping knowledge have become useless. The marketplace is much more defined these days. Some of the joy of good fortune was removed. A lesson learned is not all lessons learned remain essential.

My sage advice for working the apps is to wait as long as possible to buy before showtime and work multiple apps simultaneously. Different folks use different services. Having a partner working with you on other apps is best, chatting back and forth. Also, always go directly to the venue ticketing service as well. They often sell Broadway shows and concerts much cheaper on direct venue websites. The comforting aspect of ticketing app services is that they are fair and back up their purchases legitimately. Counterfeiting, though never an enormous problem, is rare.

The scene at Dolphin Stadium in Miami was anticipation and deal-making. Fans from both teams filled the tailgate area, and the excitement was building. The Colts and Bears had little history together. Their coaches were friendly enough men that there was not a lot of animosity towards either team. The scene outside the stadium reflected that. A couple hundred miles separated the fan bases back in the Midwest. Everyone was friendly and confident in their team's chances. It was a fairly evenly matched game except for the quarterbacks, where the Colts had a decisive advantage. Peyton Manning versus Rex Grossman? You think?

The Bears had a takeaway machine on defense and a guy named Devin Hester who put the special in special teams. Prognosticators had it as a close game. The weather didn't make any promises. There was rain in the forecast, but few thought it would amount to too much with it being in Miami. Leading up to kickoff, it was reasonably calm, overcast day but dry.

Tickets were not moving. The scalpers and buyers were at an impasse. My brothers and I had headed out to various parking lot sections and eventually came upon the marketplace. It was a large open area where they had parked no cars. Fans gathered and walked around a circle, negotiating. Supply and demand had yet to work at a settled price. Tickets were available in pairs. I needed five and was growing less optimistic. Then, there was an exciting development. A luxury suite with room for a dozen popped up as available online. My brothers and I strongly considered it. It was in the far reaches of our ability to pay, though it offered some benefits. It would remain dry if the clouds dropped some rain, and it had decent sight lines, catered food, and beer.

In the end, we decided it was a tad much for us. We returned to the open outcry market on location. In need of an odd number of passes, I had to deal with multiple sellers and coordinate them to go for my price simultaneously. I couldn't commit to one seller in a section and then find that the second guy backed out of the deal. Sellers were still in the $1500-2000/ticket range. That was me looking at a $10,000 deal, which was not a starting point. It was more or less where tickets had been all week. There was no movement. We waited it out. I prepared the kids for the potential of us watching the game in a local bar.

As game time approached, some buyers panicked, hurting my prospects even more. Tickets had found a temporary price point, but they were still a few dollars over my limit. Like a trader who showed up late for work, I stood on the sidelines, passing on several deals. I had nothing to do but wait it out. I told the kids to be ready because moments before kickoff, I would close a deal, and we would need to scramble to get in the stadium in time.

I was pulling for rain. Some light precipitation would lower the price of the tickets for no other reason than the sellers wanting to get out of the rain. Less than 30 minutes before kickoff, it had not even hinted at falling—no such luck. I cornered two sellers with four tickets together and another with two. I worked on getting a single buyer to go in with me. About 10 minutes before kickoff, and after the obligatory flyby, I committed to 5 seats for $4500 total. Yea, a pretty big number, but it would pale to the experience of watching an SB victory with my kids. Though we were not together, we were close enough in the high reaches of Raymond James. We hustled into the game.

We found our seats post National Anthem, post coin flip. The Colts kicked off to the Bears' ridiculous Devin Hester. Super Bowl history on the first play. The opening kickoff ran back for a score. Bears up 7-0, the high price of the entry fee was immediately forgotten. I had made the right decision, and we were basking in the joy of the quickest score in Super Bowl history and, of course, a positive omen.

This leads us back to the last SB I was at and the bad omen. You see? There are no omens. Winning teams stay stoic and in their present mind before things get out of hand. Teams that can take a punch. We didn't think the Colts could take it after their apparent blunder in kicking off to the best kick returner in National Football League history. They said, "We are not afraid." The Bears made them pay. Tony Dungy kept his cool, which is easy to do when your QB is one of the greatest to play the game.

Hester scored, and we led. Then the rain fell and fell. Figuratively and literally. For Bears fans, it never stopped. I have watched the replay of this game. The TV did not do justice to the conditions. They barely mentioned the rain during the live broadcast. It poured for six straight hours. Had that rain started an hour early, I would have saved considerable money on the tickets. We were getting soaked. The game looked more and more like a Colts' victory. I looked around my section of seats and noticed that only the Bears' fans seemed wet. We were miserable and soaked. The Colts' fans looked dry and smiling. The rain exhilarated them. Life is all about perspective.

Like the Colts' offense that day, the rain never let up. Halftime rolled around, and Prince was to perform (a slight step up from Up With People at SBXX). We worked our way under the crowded concourse and found our kids just as Prince struck his first notes. We did some quick check-ins and a little armchair quarterbacking before returning to the damp seats to see Prince. It was an epic performance under crazy conditions. The rain was literally purple. It was crashing down in a heavy, heavy pour while the legendary guitarist turned it up. I would later see Neil Young in a rain-drenched performance at Red Rocks, but nothing else was like Prince's performance under those conditions. He brought the thunder and the lighting, while nature brought the colored precipitation.

Most of what I remember about the second half is water. Between my brothers and I, we had three cell phones ruined. Our jeans remained soaked for hours. The drive back to Ft. Myers was even more challenging as the deluge continued and failed to cleanse our broken hearts. Compounding the loss was a very uncomfortable two-hour-plus drive along the darkened Alligator Alley in a downpour. We listened on the radio to the recap, and nothing changed. Little did we know that that night of sadness would continue for the next 15 years and counting. The Bears' lack of success in the playoffs started on that rainy evening in Miami. One playoff win since then. Sadness reigned on us that night and ever since.

Looking back, I remember significant moments of the game, the pre-game tailgate run-up, and even the week of anticipation. The joy my kids experienced getting ready for the game. The experience far outweighed the cost. It reminds me of a saying my mother used often. Once while shopping with my wife, my mom opined, "Go ahead, buy it. It only hurts for a little while."

Though it was perhaps not the best financial advice, it is true to this day. Spending money on experiences or items that will provide happiness is what it's for. My mom spent endlessly on others while providing a home of fondness and security. Her attitude of purchasing things that make you feel good regardless of their impact on your budget still rings true. Had I not splurged on that weekend with my kids, we would have had more money in the bank. Would the kids have a shining sun of warmth in their souls of memory deep inside them if I didn't? No.

In the "Psychology of Money," Dr. Rakhi Sameer suggests that "most of our emotional connections to money are grounded in our memories from childhood." Thus, like my parents, I have grown up thinking of money as a tool—something to be used for good or evil purposes. I had tried to choose good, though there have been enough times when it only served my ego, which borders on evil.

Most of the stories in this book involve money and sometimes significant sums to be available at my disposal. Was every penny I spent in these adventures agonized over? Rarely. The bulk of the time, it was not a question. Indeed, there were opportunities missed because of the overall expense. Like many investments, you must consider the risk/reward in your life. Not all cash investments need to yield more cash returned for a positive ROI. In fact, it's the making of memories that provides the most significant returns. I try to imagine a time in my future when maybe my health is waning and my children feel an undue burden of care and responsibility. The finances become part of the difficult conversation. I genuinely do not think they will say, "Dang! We would never have this issue if Dad had saved that money instead of taking us to the damn Super Bowl."

As Rickie Lee Jones sings, "years they go by." The memories linger. The stories grow in their absurdity. The time spent together always overrules the money spent. If money can make those times more memorable, spend it. It will make my mom smile.

Since that epic season, the Bears teams have wallowed in mediocrity. I only had one opportunity to share such a moment in my kids' lives. I invested in their quality of life. Sure we wanted and ached for a Bears' victory, and it hurt us deeply when they came up short. My dad passed away three years after that Bears' Super Bowl appearance. That makeshift weekend allowed my kids to spend glorious time with him and other family members. Leading up to the game itself was such glorious anticipation. A Bears' victory would have been nice, but as the cliche goes, it's the thought that counts. It was indeed the thought, action, and fluid flow of money well spent on family experiences that mattered—and what truly matters in life.

My two Super Bowl trips remain ironically connected. In my first Super Bowl, I witnessed the fastest score in history and then saw that record broken. The two teams scoring first both ended up losing. I saw the worst halftime show, Up With People, in a Bears' victory and the best halftime performance in a Bears' loss. I fell into free seats for a Bears win while digging deep into the rainy day fund on a rainy day for a Bears' disappointment. Fire and rain. Sports and life.

FOURTH QUARTER

This leads us to the family in charge of the Bears. Growing up in one, I have learned that family-owned businesses don't always make decisions based on business performance metrics. Typically, they error toward blood relations—a routine occurrence with the beloved Bears. The McCaskey/Halas family has reigned over the team for nearly a century. The Chairperson is the son of matriarch Virginia Halas, 99 years old as of this writing. George, her son, has had little playoff success since he stepped in for his brother, who was shockingly removed for incompetence.

The McCaskey/Halas clan also sits on the Board of Directors of the Bears. So after another disappointing losing season in 2021, George McCaskey addressed the media and said the Board continued to approve of his leadership. His mother and three brothers comprise the board. Go figure; blood relations rule business decisions, which is their right.

Would the Bears achieve more under new management? Perhaps. Other teams like the Giants and Commanders seem to wallow despite actual business structures in place after years of being family run. In fact, some may argue that the Wellington/Mara family ran a much better Giants team than the current corporate entity. Don't even get me started on the sad state of the Commanders' ownership.

The thing that sets off the Bears faithful is their perceived disregard for the fan's feelings. Everything is ok to the McCaskeys even when it's not. They only fired the coach and GM this time around because of media pressure. They are no doubt cheap. The team has not hired a coach with previous head coach experience except once (John Fox). Giving neophytes a chance at their first head coaching job comes with a financial discount. The Bears choose that route every time.

When a team fails repeatedly, many people are to blame. Patrons of the club start with the quarterback. He did this or didn't do that, and if he only had escaped the sacks, we would have won the game. That mentality then moves on to the defense, the offensive line, the refs, and on and on. The blame game from the fans never stops. Only after years of ineptitude do fans focus their negative energy on management. First, the coach takes the heat for decision-making. Then, after a year or two of no progress, the General Manager comes under the microscope. After two or three GMs fail the organization, the heat finally turns to ownership. The recluse super-rich treat regular people like obstacles and are ill-prepared for the onslaught of finger-pointing. Few owners have the aptitude for the social limelight like Mark Cuban. Cuban's teams don't always succeed; however, you feel he is consciously aware of their standings and has a sense of what needs to be done to improve the outcome.

Halas Hall, as they refer to the ownership group of the Bears, is in constant denial. Their aloofness appears as apathy. Fans show disgust regularly, and they hide in their palaces. Honestly, a Marie Antoinette uprising is called for in Bears' nation. The fans need to revolt. Even for one game, just don't show up. A brash boycott might get their attention. Tell them that two Super Bowls over 50 years don't cut it. Don't bitch-boycott.

Things might change with new ownership or with a great quarterback. Players decide on games. And though some of the recent Bears teams have been unsuccessful on the scoreboard, they seem to have never given up the fight. In those cases, are talent and coaching to blame?

It's a tough racket—professional football. The intensity of these games, the random nature of injuries, and how the strangely shaped ball bounces can be deflating. Teams with consistent winning profiles have outstanding quarterbacks and long-term coaches who have grown together. Even an above-average team like Tampa Bay can win a Super Bowl if their quarterback is Tom Brady. So check the stats. Teams with good healthy players and a great quarterback win.

There is little doubt that the most significant factor in a team's continued success is stability in the quarterback position. It's rare to find a team in the NFL that has performed consistently well with various QBs. The Cowboys had successful runs behind names like Staubach and Aikman. John Elway provided years of success leading the Broncos. The Giants fell off the map as a consistent playoff contender when Eli Manning hung up his cleats. The best long-term success hinges on the player under the center. Bill Belichick is the most successful coach in league history; however, his record looks a little tarnished as his QB (Brady) for that run has left. Belichick has failed to advance one round in the playoffs without him, while the GOAT Brady has won another Super Bowl.

Few positions in sports show such dramatic connections between long-term success and a single player in a single position. Pitchers in baseball have a significant impact but rarely a direct connection to a team's long-term success. Hockey goalies have an overwhelming influence on the outcome of a single game, more so than even QBs; however, the position is so prone to bad bounces and deflections that a consistent goaltender is rare. Two different goalies led the Blackhawks to three titles in five years. A core group of front linemen and defense anchored the Blackhawks' sustained drives. Patrick Kane, Jonathan Toews, and Duncan Keith were keys to the Hawks' ascension to greatness. All were playing slightly different positions. Few teams compare to the Islanders of the 1990s when net-minder Billy Smith led them to four Cups in a row. The great Canadian teams also had significant goaltenders like Dryden and Gump Worsley. However, some Hall of Fame goalies never won any Stanley Cups.

Of the 56 Super Bowl wins, 12 quarterbacks make up more than half of the total wins (34). There have been 112 QBs to start a Super Bowl, yet only 61 different men (one of them being Rex Grossman). It's hard to find a single pitcher in baseball who has won games in multiple World Series. An outstanding QB can bring you back to the game year after year.

Now, consider basketball as a sport where a single-position player can have such a significant impact. Individuals like LeBron James, Stephen Curry, and Michael Jordan have driven their teams to multiple titles. They also have played a variety of positions. One player on a basketball court can have a more considerable impact than a QB in football; however, that player can play any of the five positions. Think of Shaq and Kareem Abdul-Jabbar as centers and Jordan and LeBron as point guards if you can even say whether either of them genuinely played any one position. Didn't Magic get significant accolades for going from point guard to center in a season?

Show me a good consistent quarterback, and I'll show you a successful head coach and ownership group. The Bears' ineptitude has come at the hands of dozens of quarterbacks. During the Hall of Fame careers of Green Bay quarterbacks Aaron Rodgers and Brett Favre, the Bears have had over 50 different men play the position. (Does anyone remember Will Furrer or Moses Moreno?) Under those two stars, the Packers have contended for the NFL's top prize for years. And the Packers are owned by anybody who wants to buy some stock. If Brett or Aaron are your quarterbacks, you will win. Since the Bears' Super Bowl appearance in Miami, the Packers have won 12 playoff games to the Bears' lone win.

As of 2022, the Bears have had only three playoff wins since the 1986 Super Bowl XX victory. Immediately following that SB victory, they won one playoff game on their way to early exits from the following three playoffs. After that lone victory, the 49ers blew them out in the conference championship, denying the team a second visit to the big one. That loss set the wheels in motion for an endless rebuild.

I have been to most of those Bears' playoff losses, including the miserable "double doink" game. Another example of fans focused on the wrong thing. The rare occurrence of a field goal attempt hitting two of the three poles making up the goalposts was undoubtedly unique. However, it wasn't the only reason for the team's defeat that day. Head coach Matt Nagy made several faulty decisions. It was his first season, and many looked the other way since he had overachieved. Ultimately, his poor clock management and questionable decisions forced the field goal attempt that rattled around the sports' world.

General manager Ryan Pace made a bonehead decision at the beginning of the season. Despite knowing Soldier Field inside out, he determined that Robbie Gould could no longer be the field goal kicker. After leaving the Bears, Gould appeared in a number of playoff games and has never missed a playoff field goal. Never. As of this writing he is 29 for 29.

The Bears never recovered from that kick of misfortune. A couple of years later, most associated with the team worked in different cities for different teams. Everyone was gone except the owners.

What needs to be improved is effective oversight. The CEO needs to look at those fine details and point them out to the coach. "Hey, tough break on the missed field goal to advance in the playoffs, but... Why was it even that close? Are there things we could have done earlier in the game? Can we assess our decision-making process? What mitigating circumstances caused us to lose to a team we should have crushed by the 10-point spread Vegas suggested we should?"

That is the role of the CEO in a business as well. You want to appreciate one's success, be it management or sales, marketing, or whatever. The actual test comes in improving. Not leaving the ship to itself to chart its way amongst ever-changing seas. The Bears of Nagy's first year caught everyone off guard. He showed imagination on offense and had a great defensive coordinator in Vic Fangio. Fangio left, and management thought we were ok.

The Bears' outlook changed with the new coordinator, and management didn't respond. We needed a leader to reassess and say the 12-4 record and a playoff trip are good, but we can and need to do better. So how do we get there? Fangio's replacement, Chuck Pagano, emphasized a "bend, don't break" strategy instead of a takeaway mentality. Did our offense need to adjust by becoming more of a ball control versus a quick strike? There were no changes in the offense's identity.

Bosses need to see trends. Like what the Blackhawks missed when Bobby Hull created hockey free agency. Management should have red-flagged some of the 12-4 team's weaknesses. Teams figured out Nagy's offensive schemes early in games, while he did nothing to change in game. Look at the second-half scoring in Nagy's second year. There were little to no adjustments. I should say there were plenty of adjustments, but they came from the other team. Nagy refused, and so did his management to evaluate what was truly happening on the field. Nagy would continually say the team was looking for its identity. Isn't that the head coach's and management's job to determine? There are errors to find even in the successes.

I once had a sales trainer who said there were scoreboard managers and statistics managers. The analogy went like this. You have a quota for gross revenue or total sales if you are a salesman. That is the scoreboard. At the end of the month, quarter, or year, you look at that number and know the score. That's a scoreboard mentality.

The statistics manager focuses on more inner aspects of the performance. They look at the finer stats of the team's performance. Let's say a team won a game 21-7. The fans and players can revel in the victory. Genuine leaders need to ask, since we ran back two kicks, had a pick-six, and recovered four fumbles (all rare occasions), how come we didn't win the game 48-7? The team won, but was it a repeatable victory strategy or a one-off?

Effective management looks inside the numbers to chart development. Do we need to improve third-down conversions or yards gained on first down? Did we self-destruct a few drives with asinine penalties? Did we fail in the red zone? If so, what might we do to prevent such failures in the future?

Does our football team have that kind of feedback? Does upper management provide impactful guidance? Or does the owner say, "Mom is pissed." (An actual quote from Bears CEO George McCaskey about his mother, the team's matriarch, after another miserable season.) The Bears need owners to pay attention and not just get pissed. Provide actual hands-on leadership by explaining the plan. Owners need to look over the horizon and identify obstacles, and plan. The point is to be leaders. The Bears' owners react. They need to act.

The Bears are planning an exodus out of Chicago into the northern suburbs. This could become a defining moment of transition for many fans. I predict there will be a new NFL team in our city. They will split our loyalties like baseball. Personally, the move will cost me additional hours of travel on game day. I am unlikely to attend as many games. I have been at every Chicago sports facility's inaugural game in the last 40 years, from the new Comiskey Park and Chicago Stadium to the renovated Soldier Field. I will likely go to their opener in Arlington Heights; however, my future attendance is in doubt. I like the prospect of a new beginning. With the Bears, we can only hope we are on the cusp of one; however, history shows that we are in for a continued nightmare with how ownership has been.

Being a Bears' fan is to be proud of where you are from. Family traditions develop and solidify around supporting your football team. Football Sundays in Chicago are ritual. Rituals connect us. The community follows this team with all its heart. That's what makes their travails even more disheartening. Following the Bears has left me drunk in happiness and, more often than not, just drunk. From their mismanagement, I have learned a better way to lead. I have taken their inability to act and made it my mission to act.

We will continue to support them in the definition of insanity. We will go to the games much the same way. Regardless of the team's win and loss record, we will still buy their merchandise and continue to tune in on TV while lining the pockets of the Halas' progeny. And we will do this year after year and expect different results because we are loyal and a tad insane. Rooted in mediocrity, it's unlikely there will be change. Nothing will change until we do. I'm tiring of losing.

Mondays after a Bear win, the entire city smiles. You can sense the elation in restaurants, offices, and public transportation. People seem to have a bounce in their steps. The city turns angry after a loss. Taking care of the Bears is like taking care of the mental health of the entire city. Granted, it's a lot to ask from an organization. That's why we are content with total victory once every decade. Time is up. Let's go out there and win. My family needs to take a trip in early February again.

Chapter 5

Well This is The Year and

The Cubs Are Real

So Come on Down

To Wrigley Field

5 th INNING

My relationship with the Cubs is complicated. I remember specific details of my first game in Wrigley Field and special moments like the first pitch I threw from the rubber in the friendly confines. But most of what I remember is sadness, regret, disappointment, and being called a "lovable loser."

That last nickname is all you need to know about being a Cubs fan. For a century, this team couldn't win a thing. Big game collapses were trials the biblical Job would have trouble accepting. Being branded a lovable loser was too much for me to take. Even

Cub players and managers seemed to wear that tag with pride. I couldn't stand it and more or less abandoned the team in my teens, much to my father's chagrin.

The Sox-Cubs rivalry of the late 1970s was the best rivalry that was never contested. The Sox-Cubs divide raged in bars and at Fourth of July family picnics well before they played each other. Even then, it took a few years before the games actually counted. From there, the family banter became a blood feud with no blood ever being spilled until A. J. Pierzynski took a punch, which we'll get to later.

The Cubs became part of the national consciousness when Super Station WGN began broadcasting their games to the country during the day in the infancy of cable. With minimal live programming in the afternoons, the Cubs became the sweethearts of middle America despite their inability to win anything significant.

They were a rising phenomenon, and they hired the comet keeper, Harry Caray. They hijacked him from the White Sox in the biggest heist in the rivalry's history. We now believe the Eloy Jimenez trade is a deposit on what the Cubs still owe Sox fans after the Caray steal. It's hard now for many Chicago and national sports fans to remember that Harry Caray was the Sox announcer before he was the Cubs' ambassador to the planet. (Or that he started with the St Louis Cardinals until he screwed his way out of that job. But we leave that for his biographers to explore).

To me and a generation of Southside fans, Harry was our guy, first. We reveled in his drunkenness and mispronunciations well before he entered the national consciousness. His pairing with goofball Jimmy Piersall for a few years on Sox TV broadcasts was epic. The two might as well have been the role models for Wayne and Garth of *Wayne's World*, saying and doing whatever they wanted during the broadcast as if no one was listening. Caray's in-between pitches stories were often a travel guide to bars and restaurants in Chicago. Piersall added piercing commentary about players' attitudes and efforts, often in derogatory terms. These two knew baseball but not limits. Caray's exploits were the gold standard for what we tried to achieve in the city at night. Caray once said he kept drinking because he feared the hangover if he stopped. That kind of attitude resonated with us Sox fans. He was Southside, indeed. Then, he became the premier director of tourism for Chicago. More people than ever visited Chicago during Caray's years as Cubs' play-by-play announcer. Most of them were on buses coming from Iowa.

In the 2000s, the Broadway hit *Wicked* ran in Chicago for a dozen years. It generated hundreds of millions of tourism revenue for the city—revenue used partly to build Soldier Field for the Bears. Before *Wicked*, the town had Harry. And he ate it and, well, drank it up as well.

Losing Harry to another team back in 1985 would have been devastating enough. Losing him to the Cubs was tantamount to treasonous charges for the septuagenarian. But who could ever get mad at Harry? The seventh-inning stretch singing of "Take Me Out to the Ball Game" started in Comiskey Park with Harry. It was there where he began replacing the lyric "The home team" with "the White Sox," years before Bill Murray murdered the line in his drunk rendition at Wrigley. Caray's homespun humor entertained us Sox fans, and yes, we showered with Harry as well. Bill Veeck had installed showers in the centerfield concourse of the stadium to cool off the fans during hot summer games. Now and then, Harry and Jimmy would sit in the bleachers and broadcast the game live from centerfield. You can't make this up. On days when it "was so hot, our third baseman was Melton," Harry himself would cool off with the fans in the shower. Too much fun.

Imagine a guy who connected with his fan base like that and then left for your arch-rival. It was hard to stomach. The Caray saga was one of the few times we felt the Cubs one-upped us. From that perspective, we could deal with it. Well, that one time, and of course, there was the A. J. punch.

The Cubs and Sox played meaningless spring training games in Florida and, more recently, in Arizona. These games would carry a sense of rivalry; however, the game's loser could always claim they weren't playing their best since it was preseason. Then, in the mid-1970s, some enterprising promoters created a non-binding match in the middle of the season. It didn't count in the standings despite occurring in the middle of the season. It gave Sox fans a chance to boast as we bettered the Cubbies in most of those games. The Sox rubbed it in one year by playing Michael Jordan. However, those games didn't count in the standings. Then it got real.

Those exhibition games drew such attention that MLB finally got their act together and created inter-league play. After 100 years without it. That means National League teams for a hundred years never got to see the Yankees play in person. Criminal.

The Crosstown Classic became a thing in Chicago. No longer were the battles vocal sparring in local saloons. We would now decide our superiority in an actual game with actual meaning. It was a game-changer. Since we didn't have any meaningful playoff series against the Cubs since 1906, this was a big deal. We were ready to do battle, and a battle it was.

In the 2006 version of the Crosstown at Wrigley I showed up with a sign that read, "Finally, after 100 years, a Chicago World Series champion plays in Wrigley Field!" The defending World Series Champion Sox were visiting the Cubs for a three-game set. You could say my sign was fighting words to Cubs fans who didn't appreciate the irony. A Cubs player would take the fight to the next level the next day.

Michael Barrett was a solid catcher for the Cubs and had a solid year at and behind the plate. In the second game of the series, our hero A. J. Pierzynski was tagging from third to score. At home, he ran over Barrett. Safe. Pierzynski got up and went to retrieve his helmet. Barrett took exception to the barrel roll and stood in his way. Then Barrett smacked him. Solid direct strike. It fazed Pierzynski, and the inertia of the blow sent him back a few feet. Then the fun began as Sox's mighty mouse Scott Podsednik tackled Barrett and pounded him into submission. But the truth is everyone remembers it differently.

The YouTube video is hard to deny. Barrett landed a solid right hook. Pierzynski was stunned. What's interesting is how people with unaided video evidence recall the incident. Most Cubs fans will tell you Barrett knocked out A. J. According to Pierzynski, well over a decade later, Sox fans thanked him for crushing Barrett with that punch. What? History can be how you imagine it to be.

You can select your truth. That's how it used to be. Now video and an unhealthy number of instant pictures make things very clear. Or do they? I remember Barrett's punch as having landed solidly in Pierzynski's face. Though I choose to remember that we won the game and Podsednik avenged A. J. Cub fans have an entirely different recollection. With the video, we can see what happened. We may still choose to disagree with solid evidence. The world of politics has become such an arena. Whichever team we are on shades our memory. We choose to interpret hard evidence in a way that favors our side.

The fight was reminiscent of Nolan Ryan's beat down of Robin Ventura after a pitch hit him. In the eye-opening documentary, *Facing Nolan Ryan*, Ryan states that after his sterling career (7 no-hitters, 5714 strikeouts), people seem to recall the Ventura incident foremost. A relatively civil act of violence sticks in the memory bank much longer than his mind boggling statistics.

The Sox won the Barrett punch game 7-0. The Cubs/Sox games have memorable athletic achievements (Jordan's double, Jimenez's walk-off). Yet, the number one recollection is the punch, and even that we can only somewhat agree on. Time clouds our memory, or we remember things the way we prefer. Your childhood is a fond memory of Stingray bicycle rides to hang out at the White Hen or a horrific time you choose to forget.

Your perspective taints the scene. I recall the Sox being dominant against the Cubs in inter-league play, yet the series is extremely close. Both teams have swept the same number of season series and usually tie the six-game annual battle. We think our team excels over the rivalry, but by checking the film, we realize it may differ from how we remember it. Can we accept that? As we grow and mature, we can. For me, it's been an evolution. Once, I cheered for the blue pinstripes, then I jeered them. Now, I respect them.

6th INNING

My first recollections of Cub-dom came in 1970. I was nine and went to my first Cubs' game at Wrigley Field with my dad and brothers. It was the year after their astonishing collapse. The fabled story of the 1969 Cubs is a dramatic rise and fall, like few others. The Cubs led the division by nine games in September; they eventually lost the league crown to the New York Mets. They continued a run of ineptitude that lasted nearly my entire lifetime.

It is strange what I recalled that summer day. We were leaving Wrigley after a Cubs' loss, and the organist was playing a contemporary hit of the time, "By the Time I Get to Phoenix." As we exited the vast cement walkways, I changed Glen Campbell's melancholy lyrics to reflect a Cub fan's yearning. I began singing, "By the time the Cubs get to Baltimore, we'll be dying."

It was an Al Yankovic-type turn on a lyric that exemplified the Cubs' relationships with their fans. (Baltimore was the AL Champion and expected to repeat.) The Cubs would continue to bring heartbreak; however, their fan base would remain loyal and keep waiting and waiting for them. Not that the White Sox provided many more playoff runs, they just never teased their fans as much as the Cubbies did. Cub collapses were often grand and of Shakespearean scope. The 1969 retreat was just the beginning; if that were the only one, it would have been epic enough. It hurt me for a long time.

The Leon Durham Gatorade glove error, the Bartman fiasco, the black cat game, and the billy goat curse all seemed to be perpetrated to test one's allegiance. For millions of fans, they passed the test. It's easy to be a New England Patriots or New York Yankees fan. Those teams win time and time again. And when they are down, it is only for a season or two.

Cheering for the Chicago Cubs is a lifelong commitment to being distressed. And for that, I must send kudos to their fan base. They are the definition of diehards. They have had to be die-hard in so many ways.

For many years, the Cubs died quickly, never contending and were perennial laughing stocks. For a brief run in the nineties, they threatened to end the sport's most ridiculous streak, nine decades without a championship. They'd have to wait two more decades.

After my youthful foray as a fan in the late 1960s, I moved away from the Cubs for several reasons. The perennial losing was undoubtedly one of them. Proximity to ballparks played a role and the cool factor. When Harry Caray came to the Sox in 1971, it ushered in an era of Sox prominence on the Chicago sports landscape. I bought in. As my teen years played havoc with my identity and puberty set in, I searched for a tribe. The Sox answered the call.

Since then, my stints as an interested party in the Cubs became primarily as a bandwagon jumper. I'd rarely get involved in their day-to-day machinations and only paid attention when it looked like something magical might come along. Mostly, that turned out poorly as well. Being a Cubs' fan is arduous work. The endless disappointments and occasional near misses eventually culminated with the ultimate prize in 2016. The hardened fan base achieved nirvana but not without withstanding a near-fatal collapse again.

Every time they pulled me back in, they had a colossal failure. I felt history was upon us in the 2015 series against the Marlins. The Cubs were up in the series and leading in the decisive sixth game. I had been working late because October was my busiest season for work. I was listening to the game on the radio. The Cubs were in position to go to the World Series. I hurried home, woke my kids up, and told them to come downstairs to watch Chicago sports history.

I might as well have asked them to come down to watch a double murder. With their sleepy eyes and "But, Dad, it's the Cubs" mentality, they watched the demise, triggered by a foul ball caught by a true blue fan. They, like me, stood stunned and a tad amused by this failure to clinch. My wife was upset that I woke them up on a school night and exposed them to cruel treatment. I disliked the North Siders even more for spoiling the evening. I could not fathom what this night did to their genuine fans. The debacle against the Marlins grated on my kids and guaranteed their future as Sox fans. For them, all thoughts of switching to Cubby blue dissipated that evening.

A few years previously, their vortex of incompetency sucked me in when I was home after college graduation, enjoying a summer of do-nothingness. My dad had raised the heat on my job search. More or less demanding, I at least try for an interview. I secured one with a strange farm radio company out of Elgin, Illinois—a full 60 miles from my south suburban home. Farm radio? What was that? Rural radio had no interest for me (WXRT was my love). I took the interview to appease my dad. I would have something to chat with him about at dinner.

My late afternoon interview gave me ample time to do what recent college graduates love: sleep in. Then slowly wake up in time for the first pitch of the Cubs' daily massacre on WGN. As I settled on the couch for a few hours of viewing before I had to depart for the trek for a potential job I had no interest in, the Cubs set out to tease me again. This time, the Cubs starter was throwing a masterpiece. A no-hitter, I had been watching since the first pitch. With no-hitters, most fans come about them in the later innings. There is a call out from friends and families to watch a specific game. There is never "Hey, watch this game now because there is a no-hitter." No one wishes to ruin it. So usually, the suggestion is like, "You may want to watch the Cubs game right now."

Here, I was on top of this one from the get-go. But as the fifth turned into the sixth, I realized the time. I needed to shower and be prepared to depart if the no-hitter ended. I washed and dressed in my ill-fitting suit, tied my tie, and returned to the couch. The sixth was another 1-2-3 inning; nine outs remained before history on the North Side. The internal conflict set in. I saw nearly every pitch of this gem and felt connected to the outcome. To watch a no-hitter from start to finish was the rarest of fans' vision quests. I wavered on the job interview and considered the no-hitter more critical than any employable future I might consider. In the end, my dad's voice shook some sense into my head, and I reluctantly figured I'd listen on the radio to the final innings as I drove the 60 miles for some strange interview.

The good news was I didn't miss a no-hitter. Plus, I got the job.

That job launched my career and engaged me in an industry that was on an upward trend at the time. The fledgling farm radio industry proved to be my future. I successfully parlayed that feeble beginning into a business I ran for over 30 years. A hard-ass rock and roller who shunned any music or radio genres that were not rock became a leader in radio reports for farmers. I remember hearing the hit that broke the no-no on the radio and being happy. It was an ominous sign of a future foretold. I had reluctantly left a sports moment, which turned into a career.

7th INNING

The truth is, the Cubs of the 1970s were super cool. They had very average players and seemed to finish in second or third every year. Their lineup, however, embodied cool. They had José

Cardenal, whose afro had its own elevator. Joe Pepitone was our own Joe Namath. Ron Santo, with his heel kick jump at the end of a victory, would have been a social media sensation. Billy Williams would spit a hocker and swing at it in the on-deck circle, and we had the ultimate utility man in Paul Popovich. He was a guy who had one at-bat and one hit on his first call up in the majors that made for his entire statistic line in 1964.

Popovich was a strange idol of mine. I loved the idea that he could play anywhere. He went back and forth between the Dodgers and Cubs in his early years. He became a staple with the Cubs for the decade's first half. I related to Popovich because of his versatility. I felt I could play any position myself. It also made me scratch my head that more couldn't do that. Today's warriors come up as single-position specialists. It makes them better by focusing only on the intricacies of a single spot on the field. I thought it was resourceful to be able to step in anywhere on the field.

Announcers and commentators make grand pronouncements when an outfielder by trade needs to fill in at an infield position. I say, "Hey, he's been playing baseball his whole life. You can't tell me he doesn't know how to play anywhere?" That may be ignorant; however, shouldn't a player be able to fit in anywhere for at least an inning or two?

The praise they heap on fielders for stepping in is part and parcel of their job. Do what the team needs. If you ask the players themselves, it thrills them to be on the field anywhere in the bigs. Indeed, showing up every day to play a said position should improve your ability in that position. However, you might also get bored. It might be a pleasant experience for a shortstop, let's say, in a hitting slump to move to third or second for a game. Give him a different perspective on the game and see if it doesn't awaken some creative elements in his psyche that may lead to an offensive outburst. It's standard psychology.

It was easy to fall in love with the Cubs. The pitchers were ridiculously badass. Ferguson Jenkins. Did you know anyone named Ferguson? Ted Abernathy released the ball from about six inches off the ground with the best side-arm action of all time. Joe Niekro pitched for the Cubs as a rookie in 1967 and ended his career 22 years later as a Twin. Ken Holtzman (2), Burt Hooton, and Milt Pappas threw four no-nos in three years. They even had a pitcher named Bill Hands.

The pitching staff was a cut above the rest of the league, though Jenkins stood above them all. A Hall of Famer, he won 284 games for the Cubs. From 1967 to 1974, he won over 20 games every year except one. For this budding sports fanatic growing into his teens, Fergie was grease lightning. Jenkins had one off-year for the Cubs in 1973, going 14-16. The Cubs' response for a pitcher who had 77 complete games over the previous three years was to trade him. The following year for the Texas Rangers, he won 25 games and had a 2.82 era. Classic Cubs. This was years before the Greg Maddux faux pas. Another brick in the wall for an identity-seeking pubescent boy.

The Cubs got Bill Madlock in return. However, Jenkins threw over 100 complete games after leaving the Cubs. He returned to the Cubs in the early 1980s and had a respectable ERA of 3.15 as a 40-year-old. For me, the departure of Jenkins caused my allegiance to waver ever more towards the South Side. I was becoming a teenager and felt I had the decision-making ability to choose my own way.

The White Sox countered with the coolest cat in baseball history, Crash. Dick Allen had led the league in HRs and RBIs for the Sox in 1971. They chased this stud of an athlete out of Philadelphia, and he landed with the Bill Veeck-owned White Sox. Many think of him as a home run hitter. Au contraire: Allen led the league in triples and recorded double-digit three-baggers four years in a row. The sporting world's treatment of Allen is sordid and disgusting. The baseball press shunned him despite his on-field excellence. He passed away in 2020, one vote short of the Hall of Fame.

Allen's picture on the cover of *Sports Illustrated*, in the Sox dugout juggling baseballs and smoking a cigarette, is one of those photos as a youth you never forget. It defined 'cool.' To paraphrase a Supreme Court Justice, "I don't know how to define cool, but I know it when I see it." The shot of Allen on the June 12, 1972 cover was provocative, stylish, and chill. Heck, he should be in the Hall of Fame for that photo alone. It broke so many taboos. I mean, smoking in the dugout?

Allen underscored the new hipness coming out of the South Side. The Cubs finished second many times in mostly heartbreaking fashion. Jack Brickhouse was a legend calling the games on afternoon TV, but even he sounded downtrodden. There were classic moments like Ernie Banks's 500th home run on Mother's Day (and my mom's birthday). But something was missing. The age was changing, and the Cubs seemed stuck in yesteryear: no night games or names on the backs of their 100-year-old uniforms.

Meanwhile, the Sox were having a ball with playing ball. They had night games and bizarre uniforms, which seemed to change daily. Something was brewing on 35th Street, and it all came to a head in the summer of 1977.

The year I got my driver's license, everything changed. The South Side Hitman converted me full-time. As the Cubs were missing their window of contention, the Sox emerged with a rag-tag bunch, including Richie Zisk and Oscar Gamble. The Sox also had Harry Caray, who had invited Piersall into the booth a year earlier as a guest. Piersall became his full-time partner in that fabled 1977 year. I could drive to the game and get served in the world's largest outdoor saloon, Comiskey Park. It was great to be alive.

As my baseball passions drifted southward, I kept an ever-watchful eye on the North Siders. The Cubs still put up the occasional playoff tease with some solid players in the early 1980s, like Ryne Sandberg and Dave Kingman. They also had some stinkers, like Mike Tyson. (No, not that Mike Tyson.) They were slipping as a force in the NL. During the strike season of 1981, the Cubs won only 38 games while losing 65. There was the Lee Elia era, whose tirade one afternoon resonated with many for its accuracy. They hired a new manager, Jim Frey, and signed one of my favorite third basemen of all time, Ron Cey, plus a hard-nosed closer in Lee Smith. This got my attention in 1984, but only for a fleeting moment.

Their eventual collapse against the Padres in the NLCS cemented my devotion to the Sox. I had had enough. This team with its teases. I began making regular treks to Comiskey with friends and family. My brothers and I bonded over the game at the game. We would go to a score of Sox games each summer. We forgot how to get to Wrigley. There would be no turning back.

8th INNING

Eventually, the Cubs won the World Series, breaking a 0 for 105 streak. I watched it on TV with my wife. We had started the evening at a best friend's house, an avid Cubs fan whose enthusiasm is contagious. I wanted to watch him as much as the game. Scott Donkel was wearing an undersized Cubs jersey given to him by Milt Pappas or someone. He said it was lucky. On a night like this, all the stops needed to come out. The Cubs were facing the Cleveland Indians in Game 7. Neither team had won a World Series in decades.

The Cubs had uncharacteristically come back from a three games to one deficit to force the winner take all game. It was a night set up for the ultimate Cubs' fan dream. I felt they would win, so I ventured out to Scott's. A Cubs' championship would thrill him. My wife and I had to leave before it was over. We dreaded the outcome would leave Scott suicidal.

The Cubs had blown another lead in a pivotal deciding game, and the ghosts of all those failed games raised their head once more. If an artist were to paint the moment, it would look something like Dante's inferno with goats, Gatorade bottles, and Lee Elia screaming as black cats flew out of his mouth. The Indians had staged a comeback that, if it succeeded, would rival the most significant fall ever for the Cubs. Then Mother Nature intervened.

The Cubs had been in command of the game since a Dexter Fowler home run in the first. A Javier Baez home run and an aggressive running play by Kris Bryant in the fifth gave the visitors a 5-1 lead. The Indians clawed back after a rare miscue by Cubs old man catcher David Ross. With the score at 5-3 Ross, now the team's manager, redeemed himself and hit a home run in the top of the sixth. He became the oldest man ever to homer in the series at 39. It was the last official at-bat of his career.

With a commanding 6-3 lead, the Cubs cruised to the bottom of the eight when another Cubs' shortstop opened the floodgates. With two outs and Jon Lester pitching in a rare relief appearance, Addison Russell couldn't make a play on a ground ball. Cubs' manager Joe Maddon (my look-alike) made a move he may have regretted forever. He brought in Adonis Chapman in relief. Maddon had worked Chapman to the bone in the series, including what many considered unnecessary work in Game 6. Chapman gave up a run-scoring double and two-run shot to no name Rajai Davis. The hit cleared the left-field wall by less than a foot. The Cubs threatened in the ninth but came up empty, as did the Indians against a gassed Chapman.

During the commercial break, it started to pour. When the Fox TV broadcast returned, the tarps were being pulled and the umpires suspended play. It was God creating some dramatic effect. The two teams retreated to their respective clubhouses to commensurate. The rain looked so heavy; I thought the delay would be hours, and after witnessing a partial collapse of the Cubs, I bailed on my friend and the Cubs. My wife and I headed for the exits. Had the rain not fallen, we would have ridden the game out with Scott and his wife Nan to console them. Had the rain not fallen, we would have been needed.

With two epic curses at stake, the teams returned from the rain delay to play the most incredible inning in the history of baseball. Much like the Cub loyalist, Indian fans have been blaming phenomena of their own for the team's failed attempts to win the World Series. Most seem to settle on a doomed trade in 1960 of star Ricky Colavito as a primary cause of their numerous jinxes. The two teams had a combined 170 years of frustration. Something had to give. Both teams couldn't lose, could they?

The Cubs' tenth started well. Kyle Schwarber, who did not have a single hit in the regular season after being sidelined with a knee ligament injury, led off with a single. Then came two crucial coaching decisions. Maddon lifted Schwarber for a pinch-runner Albert Almora. This decision proved beneficial when Almora tagged on a fly-out to take second base. Then the Indian's manager Terry Francona choose to give Anthony Rizzo an intentional walk. That decision backfired when Ben Zobrist doubled home Almora for a Cubs' lead. Every Cub fan recalls Zobrist's heroics but what followed was the most under appreciated hit of all time. Miquel Montero, who replaced catcher Ross, ripped an opposite-field ball into left scoring Rizzo from third. Cubs led by two.

Much like Gregg Blum's heroics in the White Sox World Series, Montero was a seldom-used player who had more strikeouts than hits in the regular season. This night of nights was different. It was not the same. Montero gave the Cubs a crucial insurance run. A run they would need to end 100-plus years of agony.

The Indians battled back in the bottom of the tenth when Davis, yea the same Rajai Davis who homered to tie the game earlier, hit an RBI single off Cubs' pitcher Mike Montgomery who was seeking the first save of his baseball career. Michael Martinez was at the plate for the Indians. Martinez had been what Joe Buck called a "Designated Thrower" when he became a defensive replacement for Coco Crisp. Martinez hit a slow grounder to third; Rizzo charged and threw in time to retire the Indians and the curses. The Cubs turned the tables of history. They tilted the axis of the universe.

Something had happened in the locker room during the rain delay. The Cubs got religion and dropped the burdens of the past. Returning to the field after a 17-minute delay, they regrouped, and according to legend, it was because of leadership. Justin Hayward, a free agent signing going into the season, had mainly disappointed in his first year with the Cubs. His playoff performance was not much better. He turned his frustrations into a poignant moment. Heyward gathered his teammates during the delay and reminded them they were the best team in the league all year and needed to go out and play. The season hung in the balance. It worked.

They won the World Series. Pandemonium erupted. I was happy for Scott and sad that I had left him to his own devices that once every century evening.

The party at Clark and Addison the night the Cubs won was more disbelief than raucous celebrations. People walked around almost in trances. Watching them on TV, it seemed they were someplace they never thought they would be. Nirvana can appear that way. The comeback by the team that never comes back was less like letting the air out of a balloon and more like a slow exhale by someone in mediation for the last 100 years. Euphoria reserved.

Half of Chicago felt redemption. Organically, fans brought homages to the walls outside of Wrigley Field. They posted remembrances to loved ones who never reveled in ultimate victory. From all over Chicagoland, Cub partisans cried at the makeshift memorial. They crushed Old Styles cans. Grown men were driven to their knees. It was a universal outpouring of emotions. They built the tribute wall from the purest joy. That week on Ashland Avenue, near the scene of so many sporting wrecks and dashed dreams of fans past, the current Cub nation built a shrine to those who missed it.

It was a human act of connectedness. The shared joy of the communal moment extended beyond the living. A Cub World Series win was existential. Fans were attempting to hug their lost loved ones via a transfiguration. The way a bride might leave flowers at a Mother Mary statue on her wedding day. My nephews left my dad's name there to salute their grandfather. It made me smile and warmed my black-and-white heart.

The Cubs' victory was unlike any other celebration because it contained a spiritual element. Ghosts of the many who wished for this day but didn't live to see it were present. Those alive wanted to communicate with the absent souls. The walls of Wrigley were their medium. It was a shared seance—a community seeking clairvoyance with generations of Cub fandom.

They built that Cub team like the Bears of 1985. They made three consecutive National League Championships though advanced to the championship just once. The aim was to win a bunch of these World Series things. They never returned to the dance.

The thing that got lost on the Cubs' run to glory was that they pulled the rabbit out of the hat. The Cleveland Indians had won three of the series' first four games and had two opportunities at home to close out the series: their first in over 60 years. The series, which turned into a true Fall Classic, pitted the two most prolonged droughts in World Series' history. Something had to give; for the Indians' fans, it was their hearts and backs.

That night, I became what my father always wanted me to become: a Chicago fan. My dad consistently argued the importance of being a 'Chicago' fan; a full heart could cheer for both squads. I found the thought repulsive. Being a fan means being partisan. There was only one team you could genuinely be passionate about. My loathing over the Cubs increased in proportion to my love of the White Sox. I chose a side, and I stuck to it.

9th INNING

Local media aided the crosstown conflict between fans. Chicago TV reporters and sports radio jocks promoted the stereotypes of

Cubs' fans as yuppies and Sox fans as blue-collar badasses. They continually stoked the ire of fans. The on-air talents themselves were of split allegiances. On air banter would sound like the ribbing you'd hear at local saloons about why one team was better than the other. Sox' fans looked at Cubs' fans as poseurs—attending games only to be seen. As Lee Elia so eloquently said, "Eighty-five percent of the fuckin' world is working. The other fifteen percent come out here (Wrigley)."

The magnitude of the rivalry is out of proportion to its reality. Most of the time, it's the equivalent of warring factions fighting over a fifth place finish in a six-team league. Our battles for years were verbal sparring in bars and on golf courses. We found solace simply by not being the worst team in Chicago. The Cubs failed playoff runs that preceded the Sox in 2005 were frightening and then smirkingly fun. I was concerned they might win it all before the Sox accomplished the feat. I was not too sad at their eventual demise.

Mostly, Cubs' fans take the constant beatings in stride, as genuine fans should. Their continuous use of scapegoats and curses to explain incompetence does little more than let management off the hook. They wallow in the persistent losing. That might be the ultimate in fandom. I will give them this; Cub fans are true blue.

My son recently announced his engagement to a Cubs' fan, Madison Cramer. Previously, a few nephews swore allegiance to the Cubs, but this hit closer to home. The presence of a North Sider drew immediate attention in my south suburban home. Early in their crosstown courtship, she drove to our house and parked her car in front, as anyone might. Moments later, I received a text from a concerned neighbor, "What's with the Cubs' fan in your driveway (concerned face emoji)?"

I LOL-ed and then stopped to think about it. Is love possible amongst the ruins of mutual torment? Could life's greatest gift, love, transcend the decades of spite? Might my son be enough of a man to accept her Cubbie allegiance and find everlasting peace and joy? We didn't know what the future might hold. Madison was new to our family, and the welcoming and getting-to-know-each-other stage was beginning. But a Cubs' fan? Could our little love-struck Romeo sing his serenade to someone from the north side of town?

Their love has endured, and thank goodness. The ribbing continues from time to time in good humor. Our newest daughter banters with us and proudly wears her blue pinstripes to White Sox/Cubs battles on the south side, and my son returns the favor when they watch the rivalry up north. The promise of reconciliation between the two factions holds promise. It sounds overwrought to be so dramatic about two sports affinities; however, it feels so real in Chicago. We wrap our individual identities up in our sports teams. Our collective mindset overshadows our individual striving. As Scott Galloway pointed out in his September 9, 2022, Pivot podcast, "People need the collective tissue in the form of institutions."

Being a Sox fan, Cubs fan, or Bulls fan is that tissue. However, it can't become a barbed wire fence that keeps others out. It cannot lead to violence. The players battle it out in the arena, not the fans in the stands. This time we won. Next time maybe they will. And every hundred years, my daughter-in-law's Cubbies will win. For each of us, it's a matter of erasing the lines that separate us and enjoying the sport of it all.

Sports can teach us more significant lessons about how we must gain perspective and seek to understand our fellow man. If all we see in each other is the color of the jersey they wear, then society suffers. If our identity as a fan of a particular team is all we know of one another, we might get so caught up we commit an act of violence against an individual we feel we can't identify with. It is reflected in our politics. We must get to know each other, white and black, immigrants and fifteenth-generation Americans. Look beyond the lesser things we identify with and focus on what we have in common. We must seek a deeper understanding of who we are, not necessarily who we identify with. My son can grow in love with a Cubs fan. Since I have known my friend Scott from first grade, I don't punch him if he says something goofy or upsetting. I understand him. He is more than a member of the North Side tribe. I respect him.

My disdain for Cubs has diminished as I have aged or, should I say, matured? My feelings lean much closer to my dad's, who believed you should root for all Chicago teams. To him, there was no difference between Sox and Cubs. They were from Chicago, which made them our teams. My dad exposed us to the thrill of victory and, more times than not, the agony of defeat. Learn from it, he'd say. But follow all teams and be just when evaluating. Don't dismiss a player or team because he plays for the team up north. Appreciate his talent. I was too cool for school to pay heed.

That is a regret. Great ball players have plied their wares on the North Side during my lifetime. From Ryne Sandberg to Kris Bryant, the Cubs have had their share of sensational players, and I have mostly ignored them. In my defense, it's a lot to keep in your mind. Trying to remember the Cub's starting lineup, the Sox, and the significant decisions I need to make for my business gets challenging. So maybe it's a case of limited bandwidth at my advanced age. Or is it easier to hate something than to love it?

Cheering for the Cubs is antithetical to my beliefs over the past three scores. Yet, I cannot rationalize why I despised them so much. Was it because, in my prepubescent years, they routinely disappointed? Or that as life advances, you pick sides? You need to join your tribe and follow them with religious idolatry. It all recalls a scene in the touching TV series *Trying*. A new dad must drop his allegiance to his favorite soccer club because his 5-year-old adoptive son follows the opposition. His awakening to others' points of view frees him from the prison of dislike.

For me, the valuable insight came from the marriage of my South Side son to his North Side lady. Understanding and acceptance of all. An inner happiness that says we are the same and we need to separate our tribal tendencies to open our hearts to others. We are all humans sharing space together. Can we still rib each other? Always. Should we engage in threatening and sometimes physical confrontation because someone is wearing the opponent's colors? Never.

I have heard about discussion groups where blue-state and red-state citizens get together and get to know each other. Their viewpoints don't get changed, nor do the participants switch their political allegiances overnight. However, what happens is a basis of mutual trust and respect for the countering points of view emerges. As the former combatants listen to each other, a prevailing consensus follows. No one gets hurt. People listen as much as they talk.

Identity politics can be significant. People need to feel they belong to something bigger than themselves. We feel better when our team wins. It reassures us of our decision to become partisan to a ball club. It can not become our whole being. When they lose, we must keep perspective. And realize, as they say in *Good Will Hunting*, "It's not your fault."

When the White Sox have another disappointing season, I can get angry and shout at the TV while enjoying its entertainment value. What I cannot do is make that my soul for being. I cannot get wrapped up in their exploits that I question my self-worth. To be a contributing member of society means much the same.

This tendency to over-associate with a sports team is most prevalent in college athletics. I know many alums from various schools over a wide range of geography who are a tad bit caught up in their affinity. Engaging vicariously in their school's success and failures on the field impairs their ability to enjoy life immediately in front of them. My university leads the league in alum money spent without success in NCAA tournaments or CFP playoffs. My total contribution to their success was $250 in 1984, the year after I graduated. Others, meanwhile, have shown impatience and incompetence in throwing money after the elusive victory in the big game.

In the past two decades, Texas A&M has had one moment of over-the-top success. That was when a screwball quarterback named Johnny 'Football' Manziel became a flash-in-the-pan Heisman winner and took A&M to a top-five final ranking. It was one and done for Manziel as he headed off to a nice Nike payday and a pretty shitty NFL career. During that shocking run to an 11-2 season that included a memorable victory against Alabama and a made-for-TV Heisman moment, friends would come up and congratulate me and give me credit. I'd be like, "What? I had nothing to do with it."

Too many alums would have accepted that as a sign of pride. Yea, that's my school, and it directly reflects my personal worth. I have made less than a dozen post-graduation visits to the campus that "shaped me." My impact on the football, softball, or basketball program is absolutely nil. I cannot take credit for any of their success and please don't blame me for their shameful losses to teams like Appalachian State. Would it thrill me to see them win a national championship? Yea, perhaps I'd take added joy watching the game unfold. Would I wrap up my pride in their success or failure? Not anymore.

That's the essence of a genuine sports fan. The knowledge that the game offers more than statistics and wins or loses. Though it shouldn't provide you with a measure of your self-worth, it can make yourself worth more. Your life can be richer in the things that matter: friendships and family. Watching or engaging in sports at any level enhances your life.

As Scott Simon put it in his sports' memoir, *Home and Away*, "Sports is not life, but it's also not quite make-believe. The grace, nobility, exultation and despair can be real-and then we can move on. Sports stories can be memories and daydreams by which we mark our growth like a parent's pencil strokes inching up the unseen insides of a doorway."

Friendships grew under the lights, in the last row of the bleachers, over a few beers served in ratty paper cups. Often the contest's results were secondary and now lost to history. The lasting impressions are those of togetherness and shared experiences. For my friends, the games became an excuse to frolic. Occasionally, extensive planning goes into the event prep. Other times, the randomness of saying "yes" in a split second leads to a great time. It was Dave saying, "There is no question we are going to California," that built a lifelong memory. It was Phil always answering the call, regardless of the lateness of the request. If a ticket made itself available, he said "I'm in."

These moments make up the pencil and crayon marks on the inside of that metaphorical doorway. My brothers, sister and children's growth are charted along the same jamb. In the winter of 2021, my oldest brother Rick was starting to enjoy his deserved retirement from working 100 hour weeks for the family business. Rick used his street smarts, (read College of Hard Knocks' education) to become operations manager for the now multi-million dollar chemical producer my dad humbly started 65 years earlier.   Rick found himself in Sedona, Arizona preparing his recently purchased Prevost RV for a planned excursion around America with his wife, Debbie, and his adopted daughter Megan. He planned to leave in Spring of 2022. As he lifted a battery out of the engine, he tweaked his back. The pain rushed through his entire body. He did what so many of us males would do. Take a few Advil and wait for the pain to subside. It never did.

A short while after the initial injury, Rick and his wife went to a local clinic for X-rays. The news was not good. Doctors told him to drive to the Mayo Clinic in Phoenix. Staff would be waiting for him there. Upon his arrival their worse fears were confirmed. Rick had Stage 4 cancer at the age of 65. Immediate surgery was planned. In the humbleness that defined his life, he kept the prognosis silent. We thought he was having routine disc surgery. The procedure lasted almost 10 hours as doctors removed tumors from his spine. He began chemotherapy days afterwards. His strength never returned.

He was as fit as any 40-year-old and now found himself stricken by advanced esophageal cancer that had spread into numerous parts of his body undetected for years. He passed away silently in pain just months after meeting his first grandchild, Kanerick (named for Rick and Patrick Kane) born to his son Adam and his sweet daughter-in-law Marissa. Rick had loved Neil Young until his political leanings began to clash with Rick's. Though still an ardent lover of his early work, Rick moved on to Tom Petty for his musical satisfaction. I wrote a short remembrance of him that included a mix of Young's and Petty's lyrics that I read at his family memorial. However, it was Peter Gabriel's lyrics from "The Chamber of 32 Doors" off the immaculate *The Lamb Lies Down on Broadway* that sum up my brother Rick. "I'd rather trust a man who doesn't shout what he found." An honest person searching for his own path.

In the song, the protagonist, Rael, is looking for someone to guide him through the chamber of multiple doors that become a metaphor for life's choices. Avenues you can take to lead you to a life of riches or ruins. Listening to that song as an adolescent it resonated with me. All the choices we are faced with in life, from the drugs you are offered at the local forest preserve to the colleges you might consider attending. We are all searching for the answers, the right path to choose. As a teenager you are susceptible to peer pressure and are always on the edge of spiraling out of control, down a road that only leads you back again to the starting point or worse. You seek a trusted guide.

My bother Rick was that man. He had opened so many of those chamber's doors himself and often times found himself back where he started. He pushed through and let us know which paths were worth pursuing. As Gabriel sings, "survival trains hard." Rick's escapades as a young man were epic. They were fraught with misadventures and run-ins with authorities. He blazed a trail for my brothers and I to follow with less turbulence. He was our shield as we traversed life's lessons.

Less than a year after Rick's diagnosis I went to a Bears' game in his honor. As he was lying in a hospice bed 1600 miles away, a group of his friends and I gathered at a tailgate. We regaled in some of Rick's stories and shared a beer of fondness for his life which had brought us together. It was solemn, but mostly joyful. The sun stroked down on us as we hugged away our tears at the inevitable. Though he was still alive, we all realized we would never see him again. His presence hung over the group of eight. The magnificence of sport and its ability to bring us together is what matters.

We filed into the game and sat in a row together. A decent effort from the home team found us squeezing a victory out on a last-second field goal. I made some innocuous comment about Rick tipping a pass intercepted by the Bear's Roquan Smith setting up the game-winning field goal. It was hogwash, but it made me feel good. The victory brought smiles to the gang. Sure, they all had had considerably wilder times together, and those memories crept into our hearts. A tear fell from my cheek as I hugged his buddies goodbye. We made memories on this field—some by the players and some by the fans.

My brother Rick and I went to numerous Sox games together. It's tough to remember them all and more challenging to get accurate facts. Those don't matter. I can not recall the opponent or the results. I remember Rick treating me like a little brother and letting me tag along. It made me feel older and more remarkable to be by his side as we entered the stadium. I grew up, if even for one day. Rick has left us now, though the impact of his gesture will never fade. By including me in the game day experience, I found myself. As a teenager approaching puberty, everything carried excessive emotional baggage. Being by Rick's side in those bleacher seats gave me a sense of pride. I mattered. When I looked out at the field while seated next to him, I remember thinking, "How cool is this?

My connections with my family grew deeper with each random sporting event we attended. I could sit with my daughter Becca at a baseball game and discuss the best time to use a change-up. With my middle child, Buddy, watching Candace Parker win an Illinois Girls State Championship on TV, I can lament the fine details of defense on the court. My son, Tommy, and I can grow closer as my dad and I did, discussing the silliness of an off-season trade while we sit in our seats, taking in the hockey action on ice. We learn to converse by sharing our sports stories. It's a lever to move a relationship closer.

Years later, those banal exchanges while taking in a game matured into significant conversations about life partners and business career decisions. The sporting events provided the catalyst for interactions. We learned to converse over a well-played game so that later our talks didn't become awkward when it mattered—relationships developed in the arena, from the stands while we were rooting for the home team.

EXTRA INNINGS

It took three days to close the largest outdoor saloon in America. They built Comiskey Park in 1910 at a staggering cost of $750,000. Eighty years later, The White Sox hosted the Seattle Mariners in a three-game stint that turned into a wake for the old lady. They played the last game on September 30, 1990. The gate alone for that game exceeded the initial construction costs. Thousands tussled for a chance to say goodbye to the palace of youthful exuberance and generational connectedness.

Eight decades is a long time to be open to anything. Comiskey Park was a rite of passage for my brothers, friends and myself. My dad would often take us not just to the games but once for behind-the-scenes access to remove the Astroturf infield. That episode led to me bringing home a 10-foot section of the turf from the first base area. I cut it up and used it to carpet the 1973 Caprice Classic convertible that had been passed down to me through my mother and brothers. It was the car of dreams. The turf smelled of rubber. A piece of Comiskey remained with me for years until that car broke down in Gurdon, Arkansas on my return from Texas A&M following my graduation in 1983.

I was there for the goodbye to Comiskey, and so was my 20-month-old daughter. No way I was going to have her miss it. The park had memories; I needed to share them even though her recollections as a one and half year old is probably nil, she was there as we passed on the tradition. My mother also came to that game along with my wife. I brought along my 12-pound VHS video camera to record the event for posterity. I felt I was being insensitive to the old building, which was just trying to go in peace, though too much had happened inside these white-painted cement walls. I needed to tape it.

We went to the Saturday matinee game so she would not be up past her bedtime of every three hours. I filmed the day's activities. I also captured the park's interior for footage I would use later in editing my tribute to the temple of my puberty. Becca was, of course, unaware of the magnitude or even what the event was. She was just there with her dad. The family tradition continued.

I turned the video of that weekend into a montage over the song "There Used to be a Ballpark Here," sung by Frank Sinatra. This got me wondering why ol' blue eyes would sing a song about a ballpark? Because it mattered. Days at the game have significance. To those on the field and those in the stands. It brings us together.

Sinatra's rendition of Joseph G. Raposo's song is a melancholy lament of days gone past. My video production is a tour of the old confines on 35th Street, from the field-level view in the picnic area to the porcelain stalls in the men's room. The last shot is of a sign that I saw near the exit. It read, "All who leave here may not re-enter." It was a fitting closing scene to the MTV-style video, yet it was only true for that building. We could not re-enter that structure again. However, we could catch a ball game again. We could share in the joy and disappointment. Or to steal the *Wide World of Sports'* opener, we can partake "in the thrill of victory and the agony of defeat."

Following the Saturday game with the three most important women in my life at the time, I returned for the last game with my brothers. After a Sox victory, the players walked around the field. As they waved, the fans acknowledge the season's surprise success and the end of a landmark facility of our collective past. Though they were not playoff bound, the Sox had exceeded expectations and gave one of the best teams of the 1990s, the Oakland A's, a run for the division crown. They finished 9 games behind the A's, yet had a superior record to the Boston Red Sox who won the AL East that year. There was no wild card. We accepted this since we had been here before. Almost.

The following April, I saw the first pitch in the new Comiskey. It was incredible that the two places smelled the same. Both places smelt of mustard, grilled onions and popcorn. No "new park" smell here. And just like that Opening Day when I was left behind 23 years earlier the Sox were blown out by the Detroit Tigers this time, 16-0. Eventually they'd turn it around and make another run for the playoffs falling short, even though they would have again qualified as a modern era Wild Card representative. New stadium, same feeling.

The cycle of the seasons for all the Chicago teams continues with mostly the same results. Much hope, few championships. It's been nearly two decades since the White Sox were World Champions, seven years for the Cubs, the Blackhawks have missed the playoffs five of the last six years, the Bulls have gone a quarter century without a Finals return and well the Bears are pushing four decades since their Super Bowl glory.

My family and I continue to go to games. My kids have taken me, and I hope some day they will take their own kids to a game. In the meantime, we continue to use sporting events as excuses to get together. I almost gave up my Bears season tickets out of frustration; however, my son convinced me to hang on to them.

The team still sucks at this moment, yet the tickets have provided me with opportunities to connect, most recently, at the game to honor my brother Rick.

The family continues the tradition with and without me. Whether it's my eldest Becca traveling to Ireland to see her cousin, Peter Skoronski, play football for Northwestern University, my son, Tommy traveling to Atlanta to see his alma mater LSU play for the SEC championship while staying with his cousins, or my daughter, Buddy in New Orleans rocking with the Saints in the Superdome, the same building where I saw my first Chicago championship, it's about being together with your community, your tribe. In Chicago, we take pride. We are not alone. Sports reveal their grandeur and allure whether as the global passion of World Cup soccer fans or Grandma bundled up in the stands of a T-ball game. We still love our games. We mark our years at the ballpark, at the tailgates, in the arena. It's not the wins and the losses, but the ties that bind.

THE BOX SCORE

Acknowledgments

This tale of the tape begins and ends with my wife, Edie. A divine soul who always told me, "You do you." Her patience and understanding coupled with the best practical advice a man could ever need has made everything possible.

To everyone who ever attended a game, watched a game or talked about a game with me, you get it. The dozen best friends who made the offers and the others who said yes when it was my good fortune to have tickets. May you always be in the game. The Hogan family for letting me hang with Irish royalty. To Phillian your name means friend. To Dave keep saying yes. To Bill keep your door open. To Scott get a new Cub jersey. To Pat hang on to your ticket. To Greg thanks for walking into my office with a miracle.

Brothers, can I bring anything to the tailgate?

To my children for showing up on the field of play. Every time on the court, you gave everything you had. Keep it up. You get it.

To Cindy Dobrez the world's greatest librarian. Your insight and guidance will never be forgotten. I am forever indebted. To Dan Cattau you added depth to this tale. To MZ for the encouragement and the hard truths. Goldy you of golden voice. Katie Sullivan, you are a creative genius. To Bob Skoronski, you finished it and that told me all I needed to know. Thanks for taking the time. Rich at Bookies for your guidance.

To Mom for cheering for me from the kitchen window. To Dad for Game Seven and so much more.

tdobrez@codradiolle.com

Tom Dobrez - 708-267-4540

CPSIA information can be obtained
at www.ICGtesting.com
Printed in the USA
BVHW050247110523
663881BV00003B/6